TRAINING FOR REIGNING

TRAINING FOR REIGNING

RICK GODWIN

Charisma
HOUSE
A STRANG COMPANY

TRAINING FOR REIGNING by Rick Godwin
Published by Charisma House
A Strang Company
600 Rinehart Road
Lake Mary, Florida 32746
www.charismahouse.com

Unless otherwise noted, all Scripture quotations are from the
King James Version of the Bible.

Scripture quotations marked NAS are taken from the New
American Standard Bible, copyright © 1960, 1962, 1963,
1968, 1971, 1972, 1973, 1975, 1977 by the Lockman
Foundation. Used by permission.

LIBRARY OF CONGRESS CATALOGING-IN-PUBLICATION DATA:
Godwin, Rick.
      Training for reigning/by Rick Godwin.
            p.   cm.
        ISBN: 0-88419-461-2 (pbk.)
1. Christian life. 2. Victory in the Bible. 3. Millennium.
I.   Title.
BV4501.2.G596 1998   97-47372
248.4—dc21   CIP

06 07 08 09 10 — 12 11 10 9 8
Printed in the United States of America

CONTENTS

CHAPTER ONE
BETHLEHEM: FAITHFUL IN NATURAL THINGS /1

CHAPTER TWO
ADULLAM: FAITHFUL IN NEED /42

FOREWORD

RICK GODWIN is anointed of the Lord to shake us out of our religious traditions and bring the power of the Word back into focus.

Knowing the author of this book the way I do enables me to say that you are about to receive some powerful growth material! God has gifted Rick in a unique way to help you grow in the things of God. As a husband, father, pastor, and teacher, he is living out the message of this book.

If you want to stay in mediocrity and powerless ritual, don't read these pages! You will be greatly challenged by these scriptural insights to grow into a real spiritual lifestyle, which Jesus taught for all of His disciples. Rick brings tremendous conviction, but also tremendous encouragement to be all God has called us to be.

In *Training for Reigning* you'll be challenged to move up to a higher level in your walk with the

Lord. You'll find out that God never meant for you to struggle through life under the bondage of defeat and despair, but He is working in you to prepare you for kingdom reigning.

As you travel with David from Bethlehem, to Adullam, to Hebron, and finally to Zion, you will be on a journey of growth and change from glory to glory. The biblical truths you receive will be a part of your walk with the Lord forever.

Jesus said in Matthew 11:12, "The kingdom of heaven suffers violence, and the violent take it by force." As you read this book you are on your way to take the kingdom by force and be all God has called you to be!

—CASEY TREAT

M Y GRANDFATHER used to say, "There are only
two kinds of businesses in which you can
start at the top: grave digging and well digging. In everything else, you start on the bottom,
and you work up."

Even Jesus began as a baby in a manger who had
to grow up and learn some things before He sat
down at the right hand of the Father. And when you
study David's life as a type and shadow of Jesus,
you see he passed through stages of development
before he ruled Israel.

> For unto us a child is born, unto us a son is
> given: and the government shall be upon his
> shoulder: and his name shall be called
> Wonderful, Counsellor, the mighty God, the
> everlasting Father, the Prince of Peace. Of the
> increase of his government and peace there

> shall be no end, upon the throne of David, and upon his kingdom, to order it, and to establish it with judgment and with justice from henceforth even for ever. The zeal of the LORD of hosts will perform this.
>
> —ISAIAH 9:6–7

What is it that the zeal of the Lord will accomplish? The birth of a Son who will reign and bring order and peace. Isaiah is speaking prophetically of Jesus, who became a human baby because His destiny was to reign on earth. He was incarnated in the flesh that He might become King of kings and Lord of lords. Jesus was born to reign! To be king was the purpose of His birth.

That is why you can't leave Jesus in a manger at Christmas or on the cross at Easter, because He didn't stay in those places! Even the wise men knew He was destined to be king when they came from the East bearing gifts. They said, "Where is he that is born King of the Jews?" (Matt. 2:2). Jesus was born to reign, and this is the great news for us: *We are born again to reign with Him.*

> For if by one man's offence death reigned by one [Adam]; much more they which receive abundance of grace and of the gift of righteousness shall reign in life by one, Jesus Christ.
>
> —ROMANS 5:17

Before we go any further I want to make it clear that Jesus has all authority. No believer has any authority in this earth except through Jesus Christ.

With that truth as a firm foundation, God is looking for a people who will do what Adam chose not to do.

Adam disobeyed the Lord and forfeited his stewardship over creation. He refused to act on God's Word and subdue the devil, exercising the dominion God had assigned him. Consequently, he lost his ruling position. When we trust and believe in Jesus Christ, the authority and power that was lost through Adam's transgression is restored to us.

> But one in a certain place testified, saying, What is man, that thou art mindful of him? or the son of man, that thou visitest him? Thou madest him a little lower than the angels; thou crownedst him with glory and honor, and didst set him over the works of thy hands: thou hast put all things in subjection under his feet. For in that he put all in subjection under him, he left nothing that is not put under him. But now we see not yet all things put under him.
>
> —HEBREWS 2:6–8

At this moment Jesus is sitting at the right hand of the Father until all enemies be put under His feet (Heb. 1:13). Obviously His feet are a part of His body, and the church is His body. God intends for the body of Christ to reign under Jesus' headship.

> Dare any of you, having a matter against another, go to law before the unjust, and not before the saints? Do ye not know that the saints shall judge the world? and if the world

> shall be judged by you, are ye unworthy to
> judge the smallest matters? Know ye not that
> we shall judge angels? how much more things
> that pertain to this life?
>
> —1 CORINTHIANS 6:1–3

Paul is rebuking the Corinthians because they were not walking in the authority they had in Christ. They were not settling their conflicts within the government of the church. He's saying, "Wake up, people! You are children of God, destined to judge the world and angels! So what are you doing running off to a court in the world that doesn't even acknowledge the truth, and certainly isn't walking in it?" What a lousy testimony!

Jesus was born to reign, and we are born again to reign with Him. If you can't get satisfaction in a legitimate case between you and a brother or sister, bring your case before the elders of your church. Submit yourself to their authority and judgment. This is part of our training for reigning.

> And he that overcometh, and keepeth my
> works unto the end, to him will I give power
> over the nations: And he shall rule them with
> a rod of iron; as the vessels of a potter shall
> they be broken to shivers: even as I received
> of my Father.
>
> —REVELATION 2:26–27

Jesus promises rulership to the overcomers, and I believe God intends every believer to be an over-comer. He wants every one of us to be victorious. He does not ordain any of us to fail. We've been predestinated to succeed. If we fail it is because we choose to fail, because He has ordained all of us to be more than conquerors.

> To him that overcometh will I grant to sit with
> me in my throne, even as I also overcame, and
> am set down with my Father in his throne.
> —REVELATION 3:21

Before we run out the door with all this authority and power and attempt to subdue the world, however, we have to understand some principles from the Word of God concerning ruling and reigning. We have to learn what it really means to reign.

Jesus had a journey between Bethlehem and the right hand of the Father. He was not born on the throne, but in a manger—a lowly, common place. There was a process that carried Jesus into all authority, and we are subject to that same process.

Legally, a believer begins to rule and reign in Christ at the moment of salvation, but experientially it is a process. God takes every Christian through steps of maturity, building character and skill into us as we go along, and He gives us more and more ruling responsibility as we grow up in Him. God is more interested in the production of character than the provision of comfort!

One of the Old Testament saints who passed through these stages of development and submitted his life to the Lord in each one was David. He lived in four places—Bethlehem, Adullam, Hebron, and Zion—and each of them represented a specific lesson we believers must learn in order to rule and reign in Christ.

If we skip any of these destinations that represent putting certain scriptural principles to work in our lives to achieve spiritual maturity, we won't make it. We can't ignore these things if we want to fulfill all that God has called us to do and predestined us to be.

But if we submit ourselves to Him in them as David did, then the church will truly show forth His glory, conquering strongholds of the enemy that no previous generation of believers has been able to bring down!

A CHRISTIAN'S OUTWARD
LIFE SHOULD REFLECT
THE **EXCELLENCE**
AND **SERVANTHOOD**
OF THE SPIRIT OF GOD
WITHIN.

CHAPTER ONE

BETHLEHEM: FAITHFUL IN NATURAL THINGS

ONE OF the most staggering truths for me to grasp is that God has declared believers like you and me who brush our teeth and take out the trash to rule and reign with His Son, Jesus Christ. Somehow we have to come to grips with the fact that we have been chosen from before the foundations of the world to sit in heavenly places in Christ with our foot planted on the devil's neck! (See Ephesians 1.)

Unfortunately our position in Christ can be so lofty and spiritual to us that we neglect to apply it to the everyday, mundane tasks of life. When, in Romans 12:2 the Holy Spirit told us to be transformed by the Word of God, He did not mean we should move to a cabin in the Rocky Mountains, read the Bible, listen to tapes, pray, and do nothing until the glory of God shines on our faces!

The whole purpose of our position in Christ is to be able to appropriate His ability to do what is right in the present time and situation—period. Doing right is not only drawing closer to God in Bible study and prayer, but drawing closer to God as we go to work on time, keep our house clean, train and care for our children, feed the dog, and mow the lawn.

The grace and favor God has given us, which we didn't deserve and can never work hard enough or be good enough to earn, is the springboard from which we walk in obedience to His Word. God's unconditional love, expressed in Jesus' sacrificial servanthood toward us, is our motivation to do righteously.

We have a desire to extend to others the same love and service that the Father extends to us through His Son. There is something on the inside of us that wants to show His faithfulness and honor to a world that's gone mad with sin and total lack of integrity. Then others will come to Him, too.

Ruling and reigning with Jesus Christ is more than sitting with Him in heavenly places and stomping on the devil's head. We have to go up, meet our responsibilities, serve others, and be a witness to the power of God working in our lives. The question is, "Where and how do we begin?"

TAKE HIS YOKE AND LEARN

Take my yoke upon you, and learn of me; for I am meek and lowly in heart: and ye shall find rest unto your souls.

—MATTHEW 11:29

2

When you get saved and baptized in the Holy Spirit, you don't get the full manifestation of all authority instantaneously. Spiritually you are seated with Jesus in heavenly places, but in the natural there is a process you go through in which God trains you for reigning.

If you strive to turn all creation around without this understanding, you will never find rest for your soul! In fact, you can destroy your whole life trying to accomplish the vision God's given you because you have not allowed the Holy Spirit and the Word to train you.

There's a great journey between being born again and reigning with Christ. We are not born again and immediately given great spiritual responsibility any more than you give a baby great responsibility in the natural realm. A baby has to grow to some level of understanding and capability before you can trust them to accomplish anything.

A baby grows by first drinking milk, then eating soft solid food, and finally leaning to eat meat and artichokes and corn on the cob. There is no difference in spiritual things. A newborn in Christ begins growing on the milk of the Word of God. The yoke you take upon yourself is God's Word.

Newborns in Christ need instruction and discipline just like newborns in the natural. They require a lot of supervision in the beginning, and you have to do a lot of things for them until they are able to do them for themselves. Spiritually speaking, this is called discipleship.

When the time comes and you see they can tie their shoes and make their bed, you can begin to give them full responsibility over those things. As my children have grown older, as they have submitted and proven responsible, my wife and I have released a little more for which they can be accountable and responsible. One day I will toss our teenage daughter the keys to the car, but she isn't going to get them when she's only six years old!

Again, the same is true in the spiritual realm of life. Baby Christians needs to be taking in the Word of God daily and submitting to discipleship in the local church. When you see they are beginning to show some maturity by faithfully attending services, coming to early morning prayer on a consistent basis, and producing some fruit in their lives, then you can consider them for positions of responsibility. After they prove themselves faithful and continue to grow in character in a position of responsibility, then you can consider them for positions of some authority.

> (For if a man know not how to rule his own house, how shall he take care of the church of God?) Not a novice, lest being lifted up with pride he fall into the condemnation of the devil. Moreover he must have a good report of them which are without; lest he fall into reproach and the snare of the devil.
>
> —1 TIMOTHY 3:5–7

The Bible advises us not to put a novice or a rookie into office or a position of authority because they can easily become proud, be deceived, and come under condemnation. Before a believer can reign, they have to learn a number of things in sequence and develop godly character.

Also, the Holy Spirit is not going to move on the hearts of leaders in the local church to promote someone who is a hearer and not a doer of the Word.

> For if any be a hearer of the word, and not a doer, he is like unto a man beholding his natural face in a glass: For he beholdeth himself, and goeth his way, and straightway forgetteth what manner of man he was. But whoso looketh into the perfect law of liberty, and continueth therein, he being not a forgetful hearer, but a doer of the work, this man shall be blessed in his deed.
>
> —James 1:23–25

God is looking to use and promote the believer who drinks the milk of the Word faithfully each day and uses the strength and wisdom derived from it to obey the Holy Spirit in small, everyday things. Eventually you should see that believer begin to chew on some tender meat and then the tougher meat of the Word. You should begin to see him conquer the challenges in his life and bear some fruit.

One of the greatest challenges is learning to control the flesh and become like Jesus in character, but believers tend to consider this challenge insignificant compared to raising the dead or being taken up in the third heaven in a vision. The truth is, the first thing a new believer should learn from the teaching and example of his elders in the Lord is godly character.

THE IMPORTANCE OF CHARACTER

INTEGRITY, HONOR, faithfulness, loyalty, perseverance, honesty—these things should be taught and shown to new Christians as the primary example of Christ-like behavior. They should not only be told, but they should be able to see from observing the lives of their elders that those who are successful in the Lord are not successful because they are gifted or perform miracles everywhere, but because they have allowed the Word and the Spirit to bring forth godly character.

When Jesus was baptized in the Jordan River by John the Baptist, the Holy Spirit came down upon Him from heaven, and God the Father declared that not only was this His Son, but He was well-pleased with Him. God was totally satisfied with Jesus even though Jesus had not preached or taught the Word, nor had He performed one miracle!

God was pleased with Jesus because Jesus had been faithful to study and pray, establishing a strong relationship with the Father, but also because Jesus had honored His earthly father and mother. He respected the Jewish traditions and had developed godly character. God the Father knew He could count on Jesus.

I know many men and women of God who want to preach and teach with a powerful anointing and bring many souls to the kingdom through miracles and signs and wonders, but they won't pay their bills or train and instruct their children!

If I can't trust you to drive my car, how is God going to trust you with a congregation of ten thousand members? If you won't love your wife the way

Jesus loves the Church, how can God trust you with the care and nurture of His beloved and precious children?

We have churches full of believers who are constantly looking for that great door of ministry to swing open—or, worse, they are kicking in one door after another. Yet they refuse to discipline themselves to be at choir practice on time or to skip watching a few television programs in order to take food to a family whose mother is sick.

We see the same principle at work in David's life. Until he learned to care for the sheep responsibly and consistently on a daily basis, laying down his life for them whenever it was necessary, God could not anoint him to be king.

REIGNING OVER SELF

> He that is slow to anger is better than the mighty; and he that ruleth his spirit than he that taketh a city.
>
> —PROVERBS 16:32

Many people have had great opportunities to reign, but because they don't have self-control they have lost what they had gained. If you can't control your temper, you won't be able to control a nation. If you don't have the staying power and perseverance to go nose to nose with your flesh until you defeat lust, you can forget about pulling down demonic strongholds over your city. You're not going to be placed in authority in the kingdom of God until you put *yourself* under subjection to the Word and the Holy Spirit.

7

> This I say then, Walk in the Spirit, and ye shall
> not fulfil the lust of the flesh. For the flesh
> lusteth against the Spirit, and the Spirit against
> the flesh: and these are contrary the one to the
> other: so that ye cannot do the things that ye
> would.
>
> —GALATIANS 5:16–17

So often we tell new believers to clean up their lives, but we never tell them how. Basically, we skip over the spirit realm and go right to the soul and body realms. We say, "Quit smoking, drinking, and running around with those who do!"

It is true that there are some habits we can break by our own willpower. Many unbelievers have successfully quit smoking or drinking. But to be completely free of a bad habit or bondage, a Christian cannot rule his flesh by the willpower of his soul.

To overcome the flesh, a believer needs to learn to rule it by his spirit, which is led and empowered by the Spirit of God. In this way they learn to reign by their own spirit. They must be taught that change comes from the inside out.

The biggest battle in your life is going to be in the soul realm: the mind, the emotions, and the will. That's where the devil operates. If he can get your mind off the Word and your emotions running wild, then the will can swing toward sin. The key in the soul realm is to stay focused on the Word of God; then you can be led by the Spirit.

> These things I have spoken unto you, that in
> me ye might have peace. In the world ye shall

have tribulation: but be of good cheer; I have overcome the world.

—JOHN 16:33

Jesus declared that His Word was to bring us peace in the midst of the storm. When your world has turned upside down, His Word will comfort you, give you wisdom, and inspire you to do the brave and courageous thing.

But a storm can also take the form of a temptation. In this case, His Word will give you the courage to turn off your favorite soap opera for good or to tell a beautiful, seductive woman to take a hike.

When you choose to keep your mind on God's Word, you are operating in the language of your spirit and the Holy Spirit. By doing this you are subjecting your soul to your spirit, and you have the motivation and strength to keep your body in line. By staying focused on what God says you are allowing the Holy Spirit to rule you through your spirit. This is manifesting the kingdom of God in your life. You are putting your whole being under the government, rule, and authority of God.

But when you focus on worldly thoughts and thinking, you are operating in the devil's language and subjecting your soul to your flesh. You are allowing Satan to rule you through your senses and your own self-centered thinking. You are manifesting the devil's kingdom in your life.

If a woman looks across the room, sees a good-looking guy, and her flesh rises up and says, "Oh, isn't he handsome, and my husband isn't"—it's time for her to rule her body! Or a man says, "Isn't she

pretty? Boy, I'd like to . . . "—rule your body, man!
Get your mind on God's Word, and by the power of
the Holy Spirit inside you command your flesh,
"You're not going to have that pleasure, body." Paul
said:

> But I keep under my body, and bring it into
> subjection: lest that by any means, when I
> have preached to others, I myself should be a
> castaway.
>
> —1 CORINTHIANS 9:27

Ruling our bodies doesn't mean just staying away
from adultery either. There are areas in our lives
that are not moral sin but a matter of excess or
addiction. You can eat too much, or you can be
anorexic by starving yourself to look like a skinny,
fashion model. Whether you are too fat or too thin,
you are allowing your flesh to rule.

Some people cannot get out of bed in the
morning without a cup of coffee. I enjoy drinking a
cup of coffee, but I don't have flashbacks, night-
mares, and grab a machine gun if I don't get my
coffee! Why? My body's under control. Also, when
your body is under subjection to your spirit, you are
healthier. Being on cigarettes or dope is an abuse of
the temple of the Holy Spirit, but getting rid of that
stuff will keep your temple cleaner—and you'll
smell a lot better, too!

An addiction or excess indicates an inner need in
your life that has not been healed or fulfilled in
Christ. Until you surrender this area to the Lord and
put it off by letting your spirit rule instead of your
flesh, it will hurt your testimony. It's not immoral,

but it is detrimental. It affects others and can lead them astray.

There's a war going on between your flesh and your spirit, and the determining factor is your will. That's the part of you that decides whether or not you will walk in covenant with God and resist sin or go your own selfish way. You have to determine in your heart before temptation arises that when it does—and it will!—you are going to immediately turn to God's Word.

When temptation knocks at your door, say *yes* to the Word of God; then you will have the inner fortitude to say *no* to your flesh. For example, your flesh may say, "I want another piece of pie." The grace of God will give you the strength and perseverance to slap it down with, "No! You don't need it! I can do all things through Christ, and I don't live by bread alone."

Proverbs 23:2 says that if you have to put a knife to your throat to control your appetite, then do it. Some believers need to put a knife to their throats! That knife may be liver disease to the alcoholic, AIDS to the promiscuous, prison to the thief, a lawsuit and public humiliation to the liar. But the sharpest knife of all, and the only one that will totally free you from bondage to your flesh, is the sword of the Spirit.

> Whereby are given unto us exceeding great and precious promises [the Word of God]: that by these ye might be partakers of the divine nature, having escaped the corruption that is in the world through lust.
>
> —2 PETER 1:4

You cannot please your heavenly Father or do what He's called you to do until you get rid of the weights and the sin that hold you in bondage. Jesus, our example, did not reign over the earth until He reigned over Himself. He faced and resisted every temptation known to mankind. The church has to get the soul and flesh under the domination of the spirit in order to manifest the kingdom of God on earth.

> Wherefore seeing we also are compassed about with so great a cloud of witnesses, let us lay aside every weight, and the sin which doth so easily beset us, and let us run with patience the race that is set before us, looking unto Jesus the author and finisher of our faith; who for the joy that was set before him endured the cross, despising the shame, and is set down at the right hand of the throne of God.
> —HEBREWS 12:1–2

REIGNING IN OUR FAMILY

WE ALSO have to learn to rule in our families, which means we rule the place that is ours in our family. As a husband I must reign by loving my wife, Cindy, as Jesus loves the church (Eph. 5:25). As a wife Cindy has to submit to me as unto the Lord (Eph. 5:22). As parents we must reign by training our children in the discipline and instruction of the Lord (Eph. 6:4).

My wife has responsibility for the house, and I have responsibility to pay the bills for all that she does to the house! She rules it, but it takes a lot of money to rule it. But her diligence to keep that house in excellent condition, and my diligence to pay for that house, are part of learning to reign in our family.

We train our children to reign by delegating authority to them as soon as they show they are ready for it. Our girls have been delegated as governors of their own bedrooms. They are the rulers over them. Cindy says, "Girls, we want you to rule your own bedroom—not your sister's, but your bedroom—and we want you to bring it under the kingdom of God. We want righteousness, peace, and joy in those rooms. Make them nice, clean them up, and let the spirit of those rooms be wonderful. We're holding you responsible for your rooms."

When we learn to reign in our natural families, God begins to teach us to reign in the local church family (1 Tim. 3:5). Don't talk about pastoring a church when you can't bring your own home under subjection! You're not going to be an elder when you can't rule your own wife and children. That's a scriptural requirement of eldership. A woman shouldn't lead the women's Bible study if she can't train and instruct her own children in the Word.

Furthermore, God isn't going to give positions of authority to a group of people who haven't learned to tend to their own personal business. If you have more to do now than you can take care of, don't worry about ruling the world anytime soon! You have to rule what you have right now, putting everything under the management and government of God first.

No one exemplified this truth better than David, the faithful shepherd boy who killed the lion and the bear and saw to it that the sheep were well-fed and watered every day, no matter how he felt or what the weather was doing.

PREPARATION IN THE PASTURE

> And the LORD said unto Samuel, How long wilt thou mourn for Saul, seeing I have rejected him from reigning over Israel? Fill thine horn with oil, and go, and I will send thee to Jesse the Bethlehemite: for I have provided me a king among his sons.
>
> —1 SAMUEL 16:1

Saul forfeited his right to reign as king of Israel because of his rebellion, and God told Samuel that the kingdom was going to be taken from Saul and given to another. But before Saul was replaced, God had to prepare someone to rule in his place.

We look at a lot of leaders in the body of Christ who have lost the anointing—maybe they've become impure or unfit in some way—but they are still set there by God. The Holy Spirit isn't going to take them out until He prepares somebody to take their place. In the same way David was not going to take Saul's place until God was satisfied David was ready and the time was right.

Another thing we must remember is that God chooses the successor, not us. How often do we look around and think, *Boy, that guy over there looks perfect for that position. I bet he's the one God's grooming to take Brother So-and-So's place.* The prophet Samuel had that same problem.

And it came to pass, when they were come, that he looked on Eliab, and said, Surely the LORD's anointed is before him. But the LORD said unto Samuel, Look not on his countenance, or on the height of his stature; because I have refused him: for the LORD seeth not as man seeth; for man looketh on the outward appearance, but the LORD looketh on the heart. Then Jesse called Abinadab, and made him pass before Samuel. And he said, Neither hath the LORD chosen this. Then Jesse made Shammah to pass by. And he said, Neither hath the LORD chosen this. Again, Jesse made six of his sons to pass before Samuel. And Samuel said unto Jesse, The LORD hath not chosen these.

—1 SAMUEL 16:6–10

Finally Samuel asked Jesse, "Do you have any more kids? Because if you don't, I've missed God!"

Jesse answered, "Yes, I have one more, but he isn't very important."

Samuel and Jesse are about to have the shock of their lives. How often does God choose someone for a position in the body of Christ and we all look at each other in total amazement? This is because we are so messed up in our thinking about leadership. We're looking at appearance, gifts, abilities, and talents, but God is looking for an entirely different set of qualifications.

Bethlehem, where God instructed Samuel to find David, represents faithfulness in natural things. When Samuel came to Bethlehem to anoint him, David was not out in the pasture preaching and teaching. When God called him, he was being faithful in the natural things. He didn't have any spiritual authority over anyone else, and he wasn't in Bible school. He was just being a good shepherd boy and a faithful son.

> And Samuel said unto Jesse, Are here all thy children? And he said, There remaineth yet the youngest, and, behold, he keepeth the sheep. And Samuel said unto Jesse, Send and fetch him: for we will not sit down till he come hither. And he sent, and he brought him in. Now he was ruddy, and withal of a beautiful countenance, and goodly to look to. And the LORD said, Arise, anoint him: for this is he. Then Samuel took the horn of oil, and anointed him in the midst of his brethren: and the spirit of the LORD came upon David from that day forward. So Samuel rose up, and went to Ramah.
>
> —1 SAMUEL 16:11–13

When Samuel anointed David in Bethlehem, David was not prophesying; he didn't have his tape table set up in the grass. It never entered David's mind to be king. Being anointed king was as big a surprise to him as to any of his family. He was simply on the back side of the mountain tending sheep, playing his guitar, and not complaining about it. He's not looking to take over a high position in the church. He is fully content to be a good shepherd boy. He is being faithful in natural things.

When we get the idea God wants to use us, so often we also get the idea that natural things are no longer important. "Doing dishes isn't important anymore. I'm going to be a prophetess." "I don't have time to cut the grass. I'm going to be an apostle." We try to jump over natural responsibilities to be spiritual and make the biggest mistake of all.

FAITHFULNESS IN NATURAL THINGS
BRINGS REVELATION IN SPIRITUAL THINGS

WASHING THE car, ironing your clothes, putting on deodorant, paying the bills—those are natural things, and they are important. They are important because the outward life is what constitutes a believer's witness to the world that Jesus Christ can save, heal, deliver, and make the difference in a person's life.

It's wrong to say that natural things don't matter just because we're going to have a spiritual work. The truth is, in many cases the spiritual work will not happen until we are producing fruit in the natural areas of our lives.

This principle is found in 1 Corinthians 15:44–46:

> It is sown a natural body; it is raised a spiritual body. There is a natural body, and there is a spiritual body. And so it is written, The first man Adam was made a living soul; the last Adam was made a quickening spirit. Howbeit that was not first which is spiritual, but that which is natural; and after that which is spiritual.

There is a natural body, and there is a spiritual body. Verse 46 says that the natural body came first and then the spiritual body. God teaches His children

17

spiritual reality and principles through the knowledge and application of natural principles. The natural is first grade; the spiritual is second grade. Our natural experience is a parable that discloses the deepest of spiritual truths.

If you're not faithful cutting the grass and parking the cars, you aren't going to be faithful ruling in the church. If you won't obey your parents, you won't obey the Holy Spirit. If you won't follow instructions on a test in school, you won't line your life up with the Word of God. First the natural, then the spiritual.

Paul says we get a natural body before we get a spiritual body. The natural man comes before the spiritual man. There was an Ishmael before an Isaac. Ishmael was Abraham's product; Isaac was God's product. There's an Old Testament before the New Testament. There's law before grace. There's ruling in my natural family before ruling in God's spiritual family. If you violate this truth, you're in for a disaster.

In our church if we don't find that a member is faithful in attending services, the home groups, and activities of the church, then why would we want to give them a position of responsibility? They may say, "Well, I have a powerful anointing." But what kind of heart do they have? Are they faithful, dependable, and trustworthy?

God says to let a man be proven at home before you lay hands on him and give him a place of authority in the church (1 Tim. 3:5). I don't know why that's so hard to believe! How many people get "spiritual" and then quit paying their bills, washing their cars, and totally disregarding everything else in the natural? You visit them in their home, and it looks like a wreck!

I want to walk in the third heaven, but I also want to see that the furniture is repaired, the washing machine is running, the air conditioner is working, and that anything broken is fixed. Before we go around leaping and yelling, "Shundai," let's fix the water leak! Let's get the work in the natural done: cut the grass, kill the weeds, make our houses look excellent—and be at work on time. Be faithful in the natural!

This is what I say to the Christian man whose little girl needs a new dress, but he says, "Well, I'm a Holy Ghost prophet. I don't have time for these worldly things." You're a fool! Get a new dress for your daughter! Get a job that can pay your bills and take care of your family. If you take care of the natural things, God will see to it that you prosper in spiritual things.

David washed his father's car and brought the car home at curfew, cut the grass, and ran the errands his dad told him to run. He saw that the sheep were fed well and risked his life on numerous occasions to protect them. Before he was anointed to be king, he had proven himself faithful, dependable, and courageous.

You have to face all these natural things before you pursue any spiritual victories. When the lion grabbed the sheep, David didn't have any choice but to try to kill it, because John 10:11 says, "The good shepherd giveth his life for the sheep." Not only does that have a spiritual application to Jesus, but it has a natural application to a shepherd of real sheep. He will lay his life down for the sheep.

David said, "Lion, I don't really enjoy doing this, but that's my daddy's sheep you just stole, and I'm telling you right now that you are either going to give him back or die!" As he charged the lion to kill him, God called an angel over and said, "I like that kid. Take care of him." The lion died, and both the sheep and David lived.

Another day a bear came. A lot of shepherds would have hid behind a tree and prayed, "Thank You, Lord, for delivering the flock from that evil bear." But not David! He jumped up, ran after the bear, and killed him. These weren't spiritual bears or lions; these were the real things! David knew what he had to do, and he did it well—because he was anointed to be king. You have to face your natural lions before you face your spiritual lions.

Later when the whole army of Israel was cowering before Goliath, just exactly what was it that caused David to ask the outlandish question, "Who is this uncircumcised Philistine, that he should defy the armies of the living God?" (1 Sam. 17:26)?

David could look straight into the eyes of the giant and tell him he was going to be eaten by the beasts of the field because he had received spiritual revelation while faithfully tending the sheep.

> And David said unto Saul, Thy servant kept his father's sheep, and there came a lion, and a bear, and took a lamb out of the flock: and I went after him, and smote him, and delivered it out of his mouth: and when he arose against me, I caught him by his beard, and smote him, and slew him. Thy servant slew both the lion and the bear: and this uncircumcised Philistine

shall be as one of them, seeing he hath defied
the armies of the living God. David said more-
over, The LORD that delivered me out of the
paw of the lion, and out of the paw of the
bear, he will deliver me out of the hand of this
Philistine. And Saul said unto David, Go, and
the Lord be with thee.

—1 SAMUEL 17:34–37

In going about his duties as a shepherd, protecting the sheep by killing the lion and the bear,
David experienced something you can't experience
any other way except by being faithful in natural
things. He found out that when he was faithful to
do what he was supposed to be doing, no matter
how mundane, boring, or incidental that task seemed
to be, God was more than faithful to see that he
succeeded—even in life-threatening situations.

By the time David faced Goliath, he had the
spiritual revelation necessary to meet the challenge
head-on. He left his brothers and the rest of the
army in the dust with their mouths hanging open!

FAITHFULNESS IN NATURAL THINGS
BRINGS OPPORTUNITIES

BEFORE DAVID even knew Goliath existed, there was
a time when he left his duties as shepherd to be a
messenger for his father. His obedience in this one
simple errand resulted in his becoming the champion warrior of the nation of Israel.

And Jesse said unto David his son, Take now
for thy brethren an ephah of this parched

21

> corn, and these ten loaves, and run to the
> camp to thy brethren; and carry these ten
> cheeses unto the captain of their thousand,
> and look how thy brethren fare, and take their
> pledge.
>
> —1 SAMUEL 17:17–18

Here's a command to David from his father, and David didn't have to pray about whether he was going to do it. He just did it. We have to differentiate between when we are led by the Holy Spirit and when we need to obey, doing what we are told to do.

When we're under authority and given a job to do, we don't have to pray about whether we're going to do it or not. Unless we are being asked to sin or go against God's Word, we just do it. It's not that complicated! Unfortunately the church is greatly lacking in this area.

Many people get their eyes on being elders or worship leaders or some position in the church, and they conveniently forget about their responsibilities to their families and employers. Faithfulness in the natural means you are obedient to do the mundane, everyday things without any thought of whether or not it's going to bring a spiritual reward.

You arrive at work when the boss says you're supposed to be there, not when "the Spirit moves you." Let's say you are an usher, and one Sunday the head usher says, "We're short on parking lot attendants. Would you go out there and help them today?" You don't need a prophecy or a vision from heaven to know that you're supposed to do these things!

The principle at work here is that you will be just

as responsive to the Holy Spirit in spiritual things as you are in obeying those in authority over you in the natural things.

> And David rose up early in the morning, and left the sheep with a keeper, and took, and went, as Jesse had commanded him; and he came to the trench, as the host was going forth to the fight, and shouted for the battle. For Israel and the Philistines had put the battle in array, army against army. And David left his carriage in the hand of the keeper of the carriage, and ran into the army, and came and saluted his brethren.
>
> —1 SAMUEL 17:20–22

Notice how responsible David is. He rose up early. He didn't sleep late, which shows he's diligent. He didn't let those sheep stagger around trying to find something to eat while he was away, but he put them under the care of a keeper.

We see in David a big concern for little things. He took the food to his brothers, and when he arrived at the camp he checked the baggage with "the keeper of the carriage." Little things didn't slip by him. His excitement and enthusiasm did not distract him from being obedient and responsible. This is maturity!

By the time he hears the haughty challenge of Goliath, David has already had practice in battle with enemies who were bigger and stronger than he was. He's killed the lion, he's killed the bear, and he's put his life on the line. He isn't cocky, but he is confident in God.

David is confident that the Lord is faithful and

able to deliver him when he's doing his job or doing the right thing. That's different from being cocky. When you're cocky you are trusting in yourself and your own ability; you are walking in pride. But confidence is having faith in God and trusting His ability to work through you.

When you have walked through the fire to obey God and come out on the other side unharmed, you're not cocky. You know it was His power that saw you through! When David heard Goliath blaspheming the army of God, he wasn't afraid like the rest of Israel, because he had been well prepared. He was confident he could conquer Goliath, because he had already experienced the Lord's grace in defeating the lion and the bear. He had learned the spiritual lesson that God's power is there to deliver those who believe His Word and act upon it.

David came to the battle in obedience to his father, but his father sent him on the errand only because David had proven himself faithful in his duties as a shepherd. You can see how his faithfulness brought increased opportunity—and Goliath was certainly an increase in opportunity!

To David Goliath was not a catastrophe but a great opportunity for which he was well-prepared. I don't think he knew he was being prepared to defeat Goliath or to reign as king of Israel when he tended the sheep and defeated the lion and the bear. To him it was all in a good day's work. He was just being faithful.

Your disappointments, your setbacks, your stresses, your circumstances, your problems—and your blessings—are all highways on which God can train you. Your disappointments are not detours. They may look like it to you, but they are all part of God's preparatory course of development for you. Being faithful in all you are asked to do will increase opportunities in your life.

FAITHFULNESS BRINGS VICTORY

> And David spake to the men that stood by him, saying, What shall be done to the man that killeth this Philistine, and taketh away the reproach from Israel? For who is this uncircumcised Philistine, that he should defy the armies of the living God?
>
> —1 SAMUEL 17:26

Having been trained through the everyday grind of tending and protecting the sheep, David could stand before the entire armed forces of his nation and call them to account over the Philistine who was challenging them. Without that training behind him, David would have been way out of line confronting them.

It is one thing to aspire to great things, and it is another thing to get in over your head! You can promote yourself above your capacity, and if you do, you'll sink fast. God doesn't do that, but sometimes, in our enthusiasm to learn to swim, we get into water that is over our heads. The Bible speaks of not exercising yourself in things too high for you. (See Psalm 131:1.)

That's why it is so important to be faithful in natural things. You want to take on the principality of your city, but you can't seem to keep your grass cut. I don't think you're going to impress the devil—or your neighbors—at all! And I don't think that demon is coming down either! You haven't been faithful in the little things, so you have no idea how God wants to accomplish the big things.

And women, if you didn't make your bed, pick up the toys, vacuum the rug, dust the furniture, or wash the dishes, and you've left your husband's shorts in the washer so long they have mildew growing on them, don't stand at the women's group crying, "Oh, shundai!" and prophesying about spiritual responsibility for an hour. Take the glitter out of your hair, leave the women's group, and go home and do the laundry!

Bring the kingdom of God to your everyday life! That is the Holy Spirit's message to us from Bethlehem. If you do this, then you won't get into something that is way over your head. If you believe God to help you pay the rent and utilities on your house now, it will be a lot easier to trust Him to see you through later when He tells you to build a ten-thousand-seat auditorium!

David's faithfulness in the natural, everyday things of life brought him to a place of great victory, but before we come to it, we need to consider the fact that he was not perfect! The Bible records in 1 Samuel 17:26 that he asks the soldiers, "Hey, boys, what's the king going to do for the dude that knocks this guy off?" David knows that kings always did great things for people who saved them, and he wants to know what's in it for him.

Obviously David is not completely unselfish, holy, and sanctified! He's thinking, "Is the reward really worth messing with this giant?" But this is good news for all of us who still have flaws in our character to work out. In spite of David's immaturity in this area, God still used him.

While the rest of Israel was shaking in their shoes and wandering around in confusion, David didn't come to see the battle but to get in on it. With a leader who had lost the anointing (Saul), everybody was looking for someone who had the talent and spiritual gifts to handle the situation. In the midst of all the chaos this little kid, David, marched into camp and declared war!

While the army, navy, air force, and marines stare at David in disbelief, his brothers get mad at him for being so cocky, and King Saul tries to find the right uniform for the occasion. David just goes down to the brook and picks up five stones. God didn't need a sharpshooter; He just had to have a man with the faith and courage to throw a rock.

God was looking for someone who wasn't considering his own weakness with the giant's strength, but someone who was comparing the giant to the hand that parted the Red Sea! And David was that man. He ran toward Goliath, slung the stone, knocked him out, and then cut his head off—all in a day's work for a faithful shepherd boy!

From that moment David's life changed drastically. Charged up by his incredible victory over the giant, the army of Israel totally defeated the Philistines and went on to put enemy after enemy under their feet—with David as their champion.

FAITHFULNESS BRINGS INCREASE

DAVID WAS a good shepherd, a good servant, and his faithfulness brought him increase in every area of his life. I don't know if he could see it, but by the time he faced Goliath he was moving up in the world! Most importantly, he didn't do all these things from a selfish motive but as unto the Lord.

It is not our business to try to increase our ministry. My business is not to get increased opportunities for myself in ministry. My job is to be faithful in whatever opportunities God has given me right now. If the only open door I have is the position of a deacon, parking lot attendant, helping with maintenance, fixing food, or singing, then that is all I have to do. As I am faithful in those things, God will give me more opportunities, more victories, and increase will come.

Saul was handsome, powerful, talented, skilled, and well-liked, but he wasn't faithful, and in the end he tried to promote himself. Because he was an unfaithful, disobedient, unreliable, and irresponsible man, God removed him as king. He said, "I want a man to rule My people who is like Me. I want a man who has a heart like My heart."

> And Samuel said to Saul, Thou hast done foolishly: thou hast not kept the commandment of the LORD thy God, which he commanded thee: for now would the LORD have established thy kingdom upon Israel for ever. But now thy kingdom shall not continue: the LORD hath sought a man after his own heart, and the LORD hath commanded him to be captain over his people, because thou hast not kept that which the LORD commanded thee.
>
> —1 SAMUEL 13:13–14

The greatest *ability* you'll ever have is *dependability*. You can be counted on. God likes that, and that's why He chose David to succeed Saul and prospered him in so many areas of his life. Faithfulness in the natural things reflects the heart of God.

"Silent Years" Speak Loudly

When I was in seminary we were taught that the years between Jesus' birth and thirty years of age were called "the silent years" by theologians. Why do you think they called them the silent years? Because the Bible has very little to say about those years. Nothing outstanding happened in Jesus' life. He wasn't spinning galaxies into the universe or creating novas. He wasn't making clay pigeons, hitting them with the Spirit of God, and making them fly away! Therefore many scholars call that period of His life "the silent years."

> And he went down with them, and came to Nazareth, and was subject unto them: but his mother kept all these sayings in her heart. And Jesus increased in wisdom and stature, and in favour with God and man.
>
> —Luke 2:51–52

Jesus continued to increase because He was faithful to His parents while He grew to maturity. He was not preaching or teaching, and He didn't have a tape-of-the-month ministry or a newsletter. He was not prophesying or giving seminars. All we are told is that He did what His parents instructed

Him to do. He was faithful in natural things.

That ought to encourage us! If Jesus grew up the same way we grow up, and He was born to reign, then there must be a place for you and me! What did He do? He made, repaired, and delivered furniture with His father. He ran errands, collected money on the bills, and got supplies. He was just like all the other boys in Nazareth in the natural. From the outward appearance you couldn't tell that He was different. He wasn't doing anything special or spectacular. There wasn't a halo on His head, and the star of David didn't stay over the carpentry shop!

That's why the Pharisees were so astounded when He stood up, quoted Isaiah, and announced He was the Messiah (Luke 4:16–22). They cried, "Isn't this Mary's and Joseph's boy? Hey, we know Him; we saw Him grow up. Why, He was just like all the other boys. Who is He to say He is the Messiah?" It is ironic that the Jews rejected Jesus on the same basis that caused His Father to say, "This is my Son, in whom I am well-pleased."

Jesus was faithful in the natural things of life. He was just like everybody else. He swept the floor; He took out the trash. He did the things everybody else His age did. God the Father could trust Jesus the Son with spiritual authority because Jesus was faithful as a natural son first, subjecting Himself to Joseph and Mary in all things.

HAVE AN HONEST CONVERSATION!

THIS MESSAGE may not cause you to get Holy Ghost bumps and run out to preach the gospel. However, it should inspire and strengthen you to continue preaching the gospel when times get tough, you wonder why you ever went into the ministry or dedicated your business to the Lord, and you feel like quitting. You won't fail, and you won't fall, because you understand the importance of passing the test of Bethlehem, which is being faithful in the natural things.

> Having your conversation honest among the Gentiles: that, whereas they speak against you as evildoers, they may by your good works, which they shall behold, glorify God in the day of visitation.
>
> —1 PETER 2:12

Peter said to believers, "Behave yourself in the presence of the heathen! Although they may not like you, they'll have to glorify God because they will see that you're honest and trustworthy."

If you neglect your bills, mistreat your wife, abuse your children, are unfaithful in work, or take advantage of your employees, don't put a tract on a coworker's desk or witness to your neighbors! Don't be an obnoxious patron at a restaurant, leave no tip, and then try to tell your waitress about Jesus!

Do you realize what a humiliation for the cause of Christ it is when you act disgracefully, demand everything, and give nothing? You won't pay the car dealer for fixing your car, make your house payment, or pay a brother the money you borrowed, yet you come into church speaking in tongues, leaping, twirling, and spinning. You're an embarrassment to the kingdom, and you are no blessing!

This is where the rubber hits the road. Bringing

the kingdom of God to earth is not knowing what that third seal in Revelation means. The kingdom comes with getting your kids to school on time, being faithful to park those cars and keep them from being stolen, and picking up trash when you see it. If you have a debt, you pay it; if you can't, you come before the church and submit to your leadership. You take a loss, if necessary, to do right. That's honorable, and that's what the lost world is waiting to see.

If you have two cars, sell one to pay a brother the money you owe him. You grieve the Holy Spirit whenever you act dishonorably! When your creditors visit the church and see you in the worship team or in an office of the church or even just in the pew, hollering the loudest, the only thing they will think is, *That fool has owed me two hundred and fifty dollars for a year now. Boy, if they have that kind of person here, I'm not coming back.* That is the result of your not being faithful in natural things.

God wants us to be faithful in the natural things first. Wives, be good to your husbands. Husbands, be good to your wives. Treat your children right. If anybody has to go without, let daddy go without. That's the way it's supposed to be. Whoever has the greatest authority is the one who takes the first cut when times are lean. Show honor, faithfulness, diligence, and responsibility—because this is the love of God in action.

Don't put a "God Is My Source" bumper sticker on your beat-up car with the fender hanging off! The heathen will say, "Man, you need another source!" I'd put a "Prayer Changes Things" bumper sticker on the back of that beater! Put "God Is My

Source" on your Rolls Royce. Let's get the right bumper sticker for the right car. You're giving a testimony to the world! People in the world can't understand spiritual things. All they can see are natural things.

That's why I want my house clean, my yard cut, and my car washed. That's all my lost neighbors can see! They can't see angels and the Holy Spirit. They don't understand what the seven lampstands are, because they are carnal, unspiritual people. So I want my life, my wife, my kids, our behavior, our conduct, our smell—everything about us—to be godly and excellent. Then those heathen will say, "Well, maybe that guy's found something that really works."

THREE PRINCIPLES OF SPIRITUAL PROGRESS

IN LUKE 16 Jesus tells the parable of the unjust steward who cheated his master. When his master found out, he said, "You're going to be fired." So the unjust steward went to all of his master's debtors and said, "I'm going to cut your bill in half." He endeared himself to his master's debtors, and Jesus said he was very smart.

Jesus then goes on to give three principles of spiritual progress. The following verse gives the first principle:

> He that is faithful in that which is least is faithful also in much: and he that is unjust in the least is unjust also in much.
>
> —LUKE 16:10

The first principle states that *he who is faithful in*

little things will be faithful in great things. The guy who is faithful in choir practice will be faithful in elder's meetings. And this means the reverse is true. The guy who won't pick up songbooks or clean a room won't make a good preacher. If you're not faithful with your little income, you won't be faithful with a big income.

When I was taking economics in college, we learned that doctors who made half a million dollars and couldn't handle their money had often been deeply over their head in debt as interns also. They had never learned to be faithful with a little money as interns, so they didn't know how to order their finances when they had a lot of money.

When the church I pastor was just beginning, I asked one of the brothers, "Would you serve in the office of a deacon for this body of believers?" The church was meeting in a hotel at the time.

He said, "Brother Rick, I'll serve as an elder, but I won't serve as a deacon."

So I told him, "Then you won't serve at all. If you won't serve as a deacon, you won't rule as an elder."

It's not shouting, miracles, and how many people fall down under the power of God that makes the difference on a daily basis. It's doing the laundry, making sure food is on the table, paying the light bill, and budgeting the money. All these are rooted in simply keeping your word—the foundation for success in the kingdom of God.

> If therefore ye have not been faithful in the unrighteous mammon, who will commit to your trust the true riches?
>
> —LUKE 16:11

Second, we have the principle that *if you are faithful with money, you will be given spiritual riches*. Think about it! If you can't handle money, how is God going to give you eternal riches of the kingdom? You cannot draw close to Him and get to know His heart and mind if you cannot do right with five bucks!

Cindy and I have gone through the fire on this principle, but we have stood where others have fallen, too. Before we started the church I shipped a luxury car from Germany to the United States to sell here. The guy who was working with me on the other side put six thousand miles on the car before he shipped it, but I was selling it as a new car. I had to call Mercedes Benz of North America and ask, "How much do you deduct per mile in depreciation?" To do the right thing, I had to deduct the six thousand miles' depreciation from the sale price, which came to $3,500.

A little voice whispered in my ear, "You don't have to do that! For $140 you can install a new speedometer and steam clean the engine. It will look like a brand new car." That was a clever voice, but unfortunately it wasn't God! Still I listened to what it had to say and thought, *Oh, God, is there some way we can go with the $140 deal instead of the $3,500 deduction?*

In a situation like this you find out real fast where your foundation is. Speaking in tongues or prophesying, "Thus saith the Lord," will not maintain your witness of integrity. Making a sacrifice to do the right thing is the big stuff that makes you or breaks you. You decide to be a vessel of honor or dishonor.

My wife immediately said, "We have to do the right thing!" But I kept saying, "God, isn't there any way out of this?" Honestly! I tried desperately to find a loophole or a technicality to let me off the hook. I wrestled for three days over it. Finally, after searching the Scripture thoroughly, I concluded that we should pay the $3,500.

My overseas partner didn't offer to help me or to split the cost, and I never got the money back. But when I see the man who bought the car, I can look him right in the eye. I gave him a refund at our own destruction. And do you know what? That made Jesus far more happy than my prophesying. Through this time of testing Cindy and I drew closer to Him than before, and more revelation flowed into our lives because we did the right thing.

> And if ye have not been faithful in that which is another man's, who shall give you that which is your own?
>
> —LUKE 16:12

Third, *if you are faithful with what belongs to somebody else, God will give you your own.* If you're not faithful in taking care of your parents' or your employer's stuff, God isn't going to give you your own stuff. That's why I have served every man I have worked for faithfully to help him fulfill his dream. I was faithful in his house, and when I left I didn't leave his house a wreck. I didn't mess up his sheep, and I didn't bring embarrassment to his name.

When I started working for one pastor, he had seven ministerial couples on the staff and about a

$750 cash flow. When we walked away, we left him with three hundred young married couples and a $150,000 cash flow. That man's work was better because we had been there.

Do you think I could get the attention of that man now if I needed him? Yes, I could, because I served him faithfully. I was faithful in the natural things he gave me to do. At the time there were a lot of things I wanted and didn't get, but I was still faithful in what he gave me to do. Until you can identify with the overseer you are serving, you are not ready to oversee yourself.

> Likewise, ye younger, submit yourselves unto the elder. Yea, all of you be subject one to another, and be clothed with humility: for God resisteth the proud, and giveth grace to the humble. Humble yourselves therefore under the mighty hand of God, that he may exalt you in due time.
>
> —1 PETER 5:5–6

God will resist you until you submit to authority. God put you under the man or woman with whom you are serving to serve them as unto the Lord. So you honor the elder who's over you. You honor the home group leader whom God set you under. You serve them. You say, "Can I get the punch, can I help serve this, can we stay after the meeting and help you clean up?"

In our home in Savannah, Georgia, Cindy and I used to entertain a hundred young couples. We'd be up until one in the morning partying and having a great time in the Lord, but I could always count on about four couples who would stay and help us with all the work. They'd mop the floor, clean up the coffeemaker, and vacuum the rugs. They wouldn't go home until we were through.

I'm saying all this to make the point that when the chips are down and somebody needs help, the first ones who are going to get my attention are those four couples. We might not have much, but what I have they will get. They took care of us, and we would take care of them to this day, because they served us faithfully in all those natural things.

If one of those four requested a letter of recommendation from me in seeking employment, it would be a pleasure to recommend them. If somebody else tells me they want to promote them to a Sunday school teacher, I'm going to give high praises about them, because they proved themselves. Even if they are promoted out of their gift (wrongly) because of their faithfulness, people like them are still going to receive God's blessing until they find their way into their rightful place.

If you violate any of these three principles, you will never reign or even understand what it is to rule and reign in Christ. One of the biggest tricks the enemy perpetrates on the people of God and those who dedicate themselves to His work is to make them religious instead of faithful.

An example is the guy who says, "My boss got so mad at me because I prophesied and witnessed a lot at work. Finally he fired me. Oh well, I'm just being persecuted for the gospel's sake." Get real! If you promised him eight hours of work, you give him eight hours of work!

You don't witness and pray on your employer's

time. That's not right, and you're going to ruin your witness for Jesus. Get up early and pray! "Well, I have a lot of kids and a lot to do." You either need to stay up at night or get up early in the morning, but you can find time to pray and study if you really want to do it.

A lot of people get fired because they're lazy or stupid, not because they're spiritual. They're trying to be spiritual, but they neglect their responsibilities in natural things and are no more spiritual than the heathen. I want faithful people in my church who do right, servants who put their money where their mouth is, and practice what they preach!

WHERE GREATNESS BEGINS

WHO DOES God go for when He's looking for a man? "That faithful guy right over there, I'll take him. I can give him all the talent he needs. I can give him all the ability. I can give him counselors. I can give him wisdom. I can send people who'll love him. I can trust him with this revelation. He's irreplaceable because he has a heart of faithfulness."

My wife, Cindy, is a perfect example. Sometimes she's a bit aggravating because she is so diligent, but she works herself to the bone! She gets up early, she goes to bed late, and I "praise her in the gate." You could do brain surgery in our house because everything is so immaculate. If there is anything in our home that is broken, she won't go to bed—or I won't go to bed—until it is fixed! Everything has to be right. Her faithfulness in these natural things has brought her to great promotion, and will, yet in the future.

If you don't like to do natural things, you won't like serving God. You won't be promoted if you're not willing to get your hands dirty. However, if you are faithful in the natural realm, the Holy Spirit will unfold mysteries in the spiritual real.

This is where Jesus started, and it is where David started. It is where all faithful men who are destined to rule and reign in Zion must start. Being faithful in the natural, everyday, mundane things of life is the lesson of Bethlehem and the beginning of becoming great in the kingdom of God.

GOD HAS ORDAINED US
TO REACH A PLACE
WHERE WE ARE **NOT**
HERE FOR WHAT WE CAN
GET, BUT WHAT WE
CAN **GIVE.**

ADULLAM: FAITHFUL IN NEED

AFTER DAVID had proven he was faithful in natural things, he achieved great success and fame. However, success brought David many problems and a lot of persecution. The king he served so valiantly had become insanely jealous of him and was trying to kill him, so he had to flee to a cave in a place called Adullam.

David's time at Adullam was a period when he was in great need, but at the same time the tremendous anointing on him and his past successes caused a lot of needy people to come to him for help. These people did not come out of loyalty to him or because they knew he was a great of man of God. They didn't come to help and support him in his time of distress. They came because they believed he could meet their needs.

David was being chased by Saul, and his life was on the line everyday. Yet he was surrounded by people who could only say, "Gimme, gimme, gimme," with their hands out. Nevertheless, he was faithful to serve them, even though they were not committed to his welfare, and even though some would betray him. He had to learn the principle of serving the needy while he himself was in need.

SUCCESS IGNITES JEALOUSY

IN BETHLEHEM David had killed a bear and a lion while protecting the sheep, was diligent to see the sheep were well-fed and content, and obeyed his father in all of the mundane, everyday kinds of jobs he was asked to do. As a result, God saw his heart and directed Samuel to anoint him to be the next king of Israel.

Even after he had been anointed, David didn't run out and incorporate himself as a nonprofit ministry and start booking himself at all the big churches. He continued to serve his father and to be a faithful shepherd. Then one day his father sent him on a little errand, and that little errand changed the course of David's life.

By the end of the day, he had killed himself a giant, saved Israel from destruction, and become the new champion of the nation. Not only that, God gave him a best buddy for life, Saul's son, Jonathan, and a beautiful wife, Michal, King Saul's daughter. He was really doing great!

> And it came to pass, when he had made an
> end of speaking unto Saul, that the soul of

43

> Jonathan was knit with the soul of David, and Jonathan loved him as his own soul. And Saul took him that day, and would let him go no more home to his father's house. Then Jonathan and David made a covenant, because he loved him as his own soul. And Jonathan stripped himself of the robe that was upon him, and gave it to David, and his garments, even to his sword, and to his bow, and to his girdle. And David went out whithersoever Saul sent him, and behaved himself wisely: and Saul set him over the men of war, and he was accepted in the sight of all the people, and also in the sight of Saul's servants.
>
> —1 Samuel 18:1–5

You would think David would be on top of the world, but all of this success brought a lot of problems. He is about to step into a whole new ball game!

When you prove yourself faithful in the natural things and begin to achieve some measure of success, get ready for some opposition!

> And it came to pass as they came, when David was returned from the slaughter of the Philistine, that the women came out of all the cities of Israel, singing and dancing to meet king Saul, with tabrets, with joy, and with instruments of musick. And the women answered one another as they played, and said, Saul hath slain his thousands, and David his ten thousands. And Saul was very wroth, and the saying displeased him; and he said,

> They have ascribed unto David ten thousands, and to me they have ascribed but thousands: and what can he have more but the kingdom? And Saul eyed David from that day and forward.
>
> —1 SAMUEL 18:6–9

Jonathan wasn't jealous of David. He admired and respected him because he was secure in God and in his own gifting. But Saul, who had lost his anointing from God and had never learned to find his security only in God, was very jealous of David. We are seeing the first thing that success will bring: the jealousy of self-promoting ambitious people.

Those who do not anchor themselves to God and find their identity and worth in Him alone are constantly trying to promote themselves. Their insecurity actually makes them dangerous. They become furious when they see someone being promoted who they feel isn't as gifted, hard-working, or well-connected as themselves. They don't understand what the basis of spiritual success is. You do not achieve spiritual success; you receive it from God.

> Lift not up your horn on high: speak not with a stiff neck. For promotion cometh neither from the east, nor from the west, nor from the south. But God is the judge: he putteth down one, and setteth up another.
>
> —PSALM 75:5–7

If you're faithful, in due season God will promote you. But the secret is being faithful first. David was

45

faithful, not selfishly ambitious. He was not looking for anything, had no promise of any reward, but was merely obeying his father. He was keeping the sheep—was not even invited to the prophetic conference where Samuel was the main speaker—and he was faithful.

Some of you are saying, "Well, I'm stuck back here in the nursery." You're not stuck! You're being faithful! Promotion doesn't come from anyone except God if it is right.

David's place of honor was not achieved, it was given to him by the Lord as he was faithful. Many men would have done anything to have been given David's place, but God chose him because He saw his faithful heart.

> Then Peter began to say unto him, Lo, we have left all, and have followed thee. And Jesus answered and said, Verily I say unto you, There is no man that hath left house, or brethren, or sisters, or father, or mother, or wife, or children, or lands, for my sake, and the gospel's, but he shall receive hundredfold now in this time, houses, and brethren, and sisters, and mothers, and children, and lands, with persecutions; and in the world to come eternal life.
>
> —MARK 10:28–30

Even with the great reward for sacrifice in serving the Lord Jesus, you will still get persecution for that success. With all the blessing, the houses, the land, and the hundredfold return comes persecution. Your success doesn't insulate you from problems; it brings problems, and jealous, selfishly ambitious people are something you will have to handle.

You never have to worry about non-ambitious people, because they don't care about accomplishing anything for God in the first place. But there are two kinds of ambitious people: those who aspire only to fame, fortune, power, social position, or all of these; and those who aspire to please the Lord and do a great work for the kingdom of God. The first bunch are self-promoters like Saul; the second bunch will be your covenant brothers, like Jonathan.

It is always self-promoting ambitious people who are jealous. When God's favor brings you into a place of great anointing and success, those who try to achieve it on their own will be envious of you, because it all came too easily to you. You see, if you are not selfishly ambitious, but faithful, success comes easy. You just walk into it.

The guy who is sweating, huffing, puffing, and striving to get ahead, who is conniving and manipulating his way into friendships that are "advantageous" to him, never can seem to get it all. He's trying to achieve, whereas the faithful man waits for promotion, which comes from God, and God makes it easy for him.

> For my yoke is easy, and my burden is light.
> —MATTHEW 11:30

My yoke is what? Easy! And My burden is light. Now don't get the idea that I'm saying you don't have to work and obey God in what you are doing! The lesson of Bethlehem is faithfulness, and that

47

means making some sacrifices and doing some sweating. But there is a big difference between being an insecure workaholic and doing all things as unto the Lord in faith.

There is also a very thin line between vision and selfish ambition. To a lot of Christians vision is nothing more than promoting yourself and the works of the flesh. One guy has all his security in God and knows that if he's faithful the vision God's given him will come to pass. Another guy is just ambitiously carrying out his own vision.

The first guy is blessed by God, and he's not all stressed and burned out. He's confident his future is secure in God's hands. He doesn't bear the burden of his life, because his life is swallowed up in Christ. He knows he wasn't smart enough, righteous enough, pure enough, discerning enough, or anointed enough, so his promotion has to be a gift!

But the second guy is running a mile a minute trying to keep up with the Joneses and prove his spirituality, bearing the full weight of his life on his shoulders. When he sees the first guy succeed, he can't understand it.

There's a principle here that will save you years of worry and wasted effort: Don't try anything for God; just be faithful and He will promote you in due season. Then you won't have to strive to keep the position into which He has promoted you! When God gives you something, you know that He alone can take it away, and He doesn't do that unless, like Saul, you are rebellious and unfaithful and refuse to repent.

Therefore, when you are faithful and suddenly promoted by the Lord, don't be shocked if somebody curses you! It's part of the promise in Mark 10:30! Jesus stepped down from heaven and made Himself a servant to those who didn't deserve to be in His presence, and the Father lifted Him up above every name, angel, principality, and power. On the other hand, the devil reached up with selfish ambition and God cast him down.

The way up in the Kingdom is down!

SUCCESS IGNITES FEAR

THE SUCCESS God gives you will bring out the fear in insecure people. There are a lot of people who are not sure if their present position was given to them by God. Because they aren't confident God put them where they are, they see you as a threat.

These are people who have promoted themselves into their positions. When you move into their sacred sphere of influence, they are terrified of you, because you obviously have the hand of God on your life and are secure in Him.

If God puts you where you are, nobody is a threat to you. Nobody! And somebody else's success won't make you afraid either. Do you know why a lot of churches are afraid of the Charismatic movement? Because they're insecure in their own place of prosperity. If God's anointing you and blessing you and the power of God is working in your church, you'll never feel insecure when God blesses somebody else's church or somebody else's ministry explodes. There's plenty of His blessings for all of us.

We all need to feel secure in God, in who we are, in our identity. We also need to be secure in our placement. Are you where God put you? If you are, you'll have peace about it. If not, get out and go where He's called you to be! You don't have to have a big place or a high position, because when God puts you there, you'll have peace, and you'll prosper.

An old man once advised me, "Don't ever try to force a girl to love you. If there's no spark there, you may succeed in getting her to marry you, but you'll spend the rest of your life being afraid somebody else will steal her." I'm not worried about you stealing my wife, because I didn't force her to marry me. There was a spark and a drawing between us, and we both knew God had brought us together to be married.

If I weren't sure God had given Cindy to me, I would never be sure I could keep her. The same principle applies to anything else you want in life. Because God put me in my position, I won't ever worry about Brother So-and-So's wonderful wisdom and fatherly anointing. But if I had forced my way into the pastorate, and Brother So-and-So, who is full of wisdom and walks in a powerful anointing, becomes my associate, my fear would be exposed. I might think, *Maybe I'm not here by God's design, and this guy will become my replacement.*

In the second chapter of Philippians the Bible says that Jesus thought equality with God was not something to be grasped or held onto. Why? Jesus knew who He was! He was confident in His position in the Godhead, so He could release it to the care of the Father. He knew who He was, and He was fully secure.

When the Pharisees asked, "Are you the Son of

God?", He didn't feel like He had to prove it. Why? The fact that He was God could never be altered by what anybody said. For the same reason, we don't have to prove anything. We just have to be what God created us to be and do what He tells us to do; then He will vindicate us and promote us.

People in our church have left because they didn't get the recognition or position they thought they deserved. But if you're secure in the knowledge that you are called to be an elder, you won't have to prove it or make threats to leave the church if you are not made one. Making threats and leaving only proves your immaturity; it would be a disaster for you to have a ruling position in the family of God.

Don't be surprised if insecure people are afraid of you in your secular job or in the church. In all the various ministries, churches, and denominations where I have worked, I can tell you that it doesn't change, no matter what group it is. But I can also tell you that if God put you there, God will keep you there. He'll prosper you if you are faithful, regardless of what others say or do.

SUCCESS BRINGS ON THE DEVIL

SUCCESS WILL also bring the attack of the devil, who can't get to God any way but through you. You see, Satan hates God, but he can't do anything to Him except by hurting His children.

Where the devil sees the blessing of God, he knows where to attack, because that's where God's heart is. Your anointing and success will not only bring prosperity, but it will bring the attack of the

51

enemy. The devil knows that if he can get you, he can hurt God.

> Beloved, think it not strange concerning the fiery trial which is to try you, as though some strange thing happened unto you.
> —1 PETER 4:12

Remember, Satan will fight dirty! He doesn't fight fair. He's a liar and the father of lies (John 8:44). He'll play any part and dress up any way he needs to in order to deceive you and lead you down the road to destruction. His main objective is to convince you that he's the Holy Spirit in your life.

The devil comes to us through our culture, race, denomination, nondenomination, or interdenomination. To the Baptists, Satan's a Baptist. To the Pentecostals, he's Pentecostal. To the Hispanics, he speaks Spanish. If you are black, he comes to you through a black person; if you're white he comes with a white lying face.

Therefore you have to learn not to listen to religious jargon, but to have discernment, and the only way to achieve discernment is to know what God's Word really says. Like Jesus, you will discern the lie and come back with, "Nice try, devil, but it is written . . . "

For example, some believers listen to malicious rumors or to people who sow discord. They are sitting there passively, letting the devil talk right in their ear. They haven't read Revelation 12:10, where it says Satan is the accuser of the brethren. They just sit there thinking the Holy Spirit is enlightening them!

Part of growing up in the Christian life is simply getting the Bible out and doing your homework. Just like school, if you don't study before the test comes, you will flunk the test. In real life, however, flunking the test can mean terrible destruction to you and those around you. It can mean you will not fulfill your purpose in life.

So crack the Book and start studying! Don't be surprised when the devil shows up at your door, speaking your lingo, and trying to sell you a pack of lies. If you've done your homework, you can kick him off your doorstep before he even gets started!

Success Will Test Relationships

When David began to achieve some success, it tested all his relationships. He discovered that some relationships become insecure or fade away because they are based on the person we used to be, not the person we are now. Success brings change in every area of our lives.

Take a bunch of guys who are friends before any of them begin to accomplish anything in life. Their relationships are based on who they are and what they have at that time in their lives. When success comes to one, and growth comes to another, those relationships are challenged and strained.

One man says to another, "You're not the same man you were eight years ago. You're not the same one we teamed up with."

The other man says, "You're right!" And it will test whether that relationship was spiritual or fleshly. The friends I started out with are still my friends today if the friendship was based on the principles of the kingdom of God and not on having our own selfish needs met.

When you begin to grow up in God, remain faithful in the natural things, and are promoted of the Lord, you become the agent of the Holy Spirit to do one of two things to those around you: If they are also growing in the Lord, they will recognize the hand of God on your life and encourage you in your success; but if they are just sitting around playing church, your success will put them under conviction.

If your friends are under conviction, they will get mad at you! They don't like you anymore because you've changed. When I was a Baptist, I had one group of friends; when I became Charismatic, it tested the friendships I had with the Baptists. I became an agent of the Holy Spirit to invoke change in my friends, and some didn't want to change. They liked me as a Baptist, but they didn't like me as a Charismatic. To go on with God and keep growing, I lost some friends.

David's relationship with his wife, who was Saul's daughter, fell apart when David danced before the Lord in the ephod of a common priest instead of his kingly robes. The Bible says she despised him. (See 2 Samuel 6:14–16.) Still, there was one friend who stuck with him till the end.

> And Jonathan said unto David, Come, and let us go out into the field. And they went out both of them into the field. And Jonathan said unto David, O LORD God of Israel, when I have sounded my father about tomorrow any time, or the third day, and, behold, if there be

good toward David, and I then send not unto thee, and shew it thee; the LORD do so and much more to Jonathan: but if it please my father to do thee evil, then I will shew it thee, and send thee away, that thou mayest go in peace: and the LORD be with thee, as he hath been with my father. And thou shalt not only while yet I live shew me the kindness of the LORD, that I die not: but also thou shalt not cut off thy kindness from my house for ever: no, not when the LORD hath cut off the enemies of David every one from the face of the earth. So Jonathan made a covenant with the house of David, saying, Let the LORD even require it at the hand of David's enemies. And Jonathan caused David to swear again, because he loved him: for he loved him as he loved his own soul.

—1 SAMUEL 20:11–17

When you begin to grow up in God, your relationships are going to be based on a different standard—covenant. Covenant relationships are the ones that will stand the test of success. Jonathan stood with David because God had anointed David, and Jonathan recognized it. When you can recognize someone whom God is blessing, you are recognizing God. If I honor a vessel God is using, I'm honoring the Lord.

When a wife honors her husband, she is honoring the Lord because the Lord set her husband in authority over her. Now every wife knows the Lord didn't make husbands the head because they were better, so we can end that argument right now! But when we honor those in delegated authority, we honor the Lord who set them there. It is impossible to say you are right with God when you are out of order with those in authority over you.

If I'm out of order with the elders who are authorities in our church, then I'm not right with God, no matter how anointed the Lord might allow me to be. To take this one step further, when you rightly relate to your brother you rightly relate to God, because God has established your brother. You cannot relate to God's people one way and God another way. You cannot be blind to God's people and be alert to God.

> Henceforth know we no man after the flesh.
> —2 Corinthians 5:16

Covenant relationships mean knowing each other after the *spirit,* not the *flesh.* Be careful that men don't love your flesh! That's flattery, not honor. If someone is your friend because they like the way you look, how talented you are, or how much money or power you have, it's a relationship based on need and flesh; it has nothing to do with giving honor. (This is a typical Adullam relationship.)

Jonathan's spiritual relationship with David was stronger than his natural relationship with his father, which made Saul even more jealous and angry with David. The boys' spiritual relationship was stronger because it was a covenant, where each person is fully committed to the other.

> Then Saul's anger was kindled against Jonathan, and he said unto him, Thou son of the perverse

rebellious woman, do not I know that thou hast chosen the son of Jesse to thine own confusion, and unto the confusion of thy mother's naked-ness? For as long as the son of Jesse liveth upon the ground, thou shalt not be established, nor thy kingdom. Wherefore now send and fetch him unto me, for he shall surely die.

—1 SAMUEL 20:30–31

Jonathan loved David at the expense of his own father's love and at the expense of his being king one day himself. This is covenant love—loving at the cost of everything you have when you don't get anything out of it.

And Jonathan gave his artillery unto his lad, and said unto him, Go, carry them to the city. And as soon as the lad was gone, David arose out of a place toward the south, and fell on his face to the ground, and bowed himself three times: and they kissed one another, and wept one with another, until David exceeded. And Jonathan said to David, Go in peace, foras-much as we have sworn both of us in the name of the LORD, saying, The LORD be between me and thee, and between my seed and thy seed for ever. And he arose and departed: and Jonathan went into the city.

—1 SAMUEL 20:40–42

What most Christians call love is actually *convenient love*, not *covenant love*. That's why the relationships don't last. Convenient love is loving somebody for what you can get out of them. "I love you because

you can help me." We see people aligning themselves with other people purely because it's good
for business, promotes their ministry, or makes
them look good. There's no spiritual unity, and God
didn't have anything to do with it!

When God makes a covenant with you and me,
He commits Himself completely. On the other hand,
what we do is say, "Well, I want the benefits of the
covenant, and I'll think about committing myself to
you." Many of us desire all the benefits of a covenant
relationship without the responsibility. It's like having
sex and all the privileges of marriage without the
marriage covenant.

But the sign of a mature believer and a spiritual
giant is not someone who can cast out devils, raise
the dead, and prophesy. These things are wonderful and they are part of our calling, but God is
looking for those who will totally commit themselves to Him and lay down their lives for others
just like Jesus did.

ONLY THE NEEDY

> David therefore departed thence, and escaped
> to the cave Adullam: and when his brethren
> and all his father's house heard it, they went
> down thither to him. And every one that was
> in distress, and every one that was in debt,
> and every one that was discontented, gathered
> themselves unto him; and he became a cap-
> tain over them: and there were with him about
> four hundred men.
>
> —1 SAMUEL 22:1–2

When David escaped Saul and became an outcast, he became captain over the needy. Needy people were attracted to David because of his success. We are not ready to reign in life, which is Zion, until we have compassion on needy people while we ourselves are yet in need.

You have to learn to care for needy people while you have a need in your own life. Sometimes you pray for the sick when you're sicker than the one for whom you're praying. Other times you give a man twenty dollars so he can feed the starving in Africa and do without a meal yourself. That's the Christian life! David has some huge problems, but the crowd following him is in worse shape than he is. Adullam is the stage of need-oriented Christianity in our growth as believers.

Saul was bankrupt spiritually, and everybody knew it. He had turned away from the Holy Spirit, and a lot of people had realized he was in sin. Meanwhile, David's charismatic personality and success in killing the giant attracted a lot of people to him. The power and anointing of God attract people with needs.

When your church begins to get a reputation for seeing the power of God move in the lives of its members, when you begin to have a positive impact on your community by standing up for righteousness and truth, then don't be surprised who shows up! That's what happened to David, and he became captain of the rebels, the needy, and the malcontent.

Adullam represents how the blessing of the Lord gets you in trouble. Four hundred men came to join up with David, and the Bible says they were distressed, discontented, and in debt. This was not a great crowd! This is not an army, but a mob! He can't take Zion with this group. They came to David because of their need and his anointing, seeking to get something out of him.

David can't fight with this group. They are carnal, selfish, and disorderly. They're messed up because they think David can solve all of their problems. They were not there to establish David's kingdom, but merely to get their needs met. They didn't see the greater purpose; they only saw their own misfortune.

For the most part, the people who flock to a church where the Holy Spirit is doing great things are also not going to be the nice people, but the unbalanced, sick, and needy people. Initially they are not interested in becoming like Jesus Christ, establishing His kingdom, and being a blessing to everyone with whom they come in contact.

They'll cry, "I need that music; I need that word; I need that prophecy; I need the attention of the pastor." However, God can take a sow's ear and make a silk purse out of it. That's what He did with the people who followed David, and that's what He is still doing today! Many people really don't understand that this is the purpose of the local church.

> For ye see your calling, brethren, how that not many wise men after the flesh, not many mighty, not many noble, are called: but God hath chosen the foolish things of the world to confound the wise; and God hath chosen the weak things of the world to confound the things which are mighty; and base things of the world, and things which are despised, hath God chosen, yea, and things which are not, to

bring to nought things that are: that no flesh should glory in his presence.

—1 CORINTHIANS 1:26–29

Jesus takes hopeless people, and He does something with them.

JESUS HAD AN ADULLAM CROWD

And Jesus went about all Galilee, teaching in their synagogues, and preaching the gospel of the kingdom, and healing all manner of sickness and all manner of disease among the people. And his fame went throughout all Syria: and they brought unto him all sick people that were taken with divers diseases and torments, and those which were possessed with devils, and those which were lunatic, and those that had the palsy; and he healed them. And there followed him great multitudes of people from Galilee, and from Decapolis, and from Jerusalem, and from Judea, and from beyond Jordan.

—MATTHEW 4:23–25

What a crowd! This is not "Who's Who in Jerusalem" at Jesus' meetings! He had afflicted, lunatic people showing up by the thousands. Visualize in your mind what that must have been like. We've had a few people come into our church who were demonized, but imagine thousands of lunatics flocking into your church one Sunday. You would not want your picture taken with this crowd!

Every weird person with problems came to Jesus.

Do you think that might have hurt His reputation? One of the tests of Adullam is that the devil will try to get you to quit helping needy people in order to protect your reputation. You can be discredited as a church or a believer because of your association with the strange and even evil people who like you or come to you for help.

The Pharisees, Saducees, and even the disciples gave Jesus a hard time for associating with tax collectors and sinners. The prostitutes, the drunkards, the publicans—they all loved Jesus, and the religious crowd hated Jesus because of His association with these wicked, needy people.

Thank God we're not keepers of the aquarium, but fishers of men! The church is no museum; it's supposed to be a nursery. There are a lot of stinky diapers, spitting up, crying, and fussing in a nursery, but there is also new life. We're going to have all kinds of problems; immature people, carnal people, ambitious people, and even dishonest and evil people come to us for help.

God's love is a covenant love, which means He gave Jesus regardless of whether you and I would receive Him. I don't know if you're aware of it, but you gave Jesus a bad name! When He loved you, He was identifying Himself with a sinner. But He still identifies with you, and He still loves you. Aren't you glad He does?

Walking in grace means loving and meeting the needs of others at the cost of your own reputation.

Jesus had His own Adullam bunch. They heard He was the Messiah, that He healed the sick, and they came for Him to meet their needs. They did not recognize Him as God Almighty in the flesh, and there was no commitment to Him or recognition of His destiny and purpose in the earth. Jesus changed many of their lives, but many of them walked away healed without ever giving Him thanks or receiving Him as their Lord and Savior.

Jesus' crowd, like David's, didn't know who He was or what His destiny was; they just wanted help. But in reality, all of us came to Jesus out of our need. We didn't come to Him for what we could do for Him. We came for what He could do for us. *And that's not wrong!* That's why we first come to Him.

I am not condemning you if you're at the level of need-oriented Christianity. I'm just trying to show you that you have to mature from there. A baby comes out of the womb and depends on the parents for everything, and if you've just been saved, you need a lot of counsel and attention. For a period of time, as you grow, it's perfectly normal to depend on more mature believers who can teach you how to depend more and more on God instead of them.

But these are temporary relationships. It becomes abnormal if you continue to come to church and fellowship with other believers just to get what you can get. There comes the time when we say to our children, "You are now old enough and mature enough to be responsible, and we, your parents, want you to know we don't just exist for you. You're going to honor us, and you're going to clean your room, make your bed, brush your own teeth, and learn to tie your shoes. You're going to learn to defend yourself a little bit. And one day you're going to leave home and be a productive, godly Christian citizen."

God wants you and I to be mature Christians. He wants us to grow up and say, "God doesn't exist for me; I exist for the Lord—to be an instrument through whom God displays His mercy, compassion, and glory to the world." We must go beyond "Gimme, gimme, gimme, what can You do for me, Lord?" to "What can I do for You, Lord?" Those who make it through the process of growing up make it to Zion, the place of ruling and reigning in Christ.

BEING A GODLY EXAMPLE AMONG REBELS

WE HAVE seen that even when you are faithful in the natural things, have achieved some success, and have been put in a position of leadership, the testing doesn't stop. Problems and needs are going to come. How you handle those problems and whether or not you trust God to meet those needs is going to be an example to all who are following you. The sheep always want to see if the shepherd practices what he preaches!

One of the hardest things to do in the ministry is to keep from being influenced or changed by people who come to you for help. David was around malcontents, but he didn't become a malcontent. He was around rebels, but he didn't become rebellious. He had to resist their rebellion and show forth an attitude of submission so they would change into godly men.

David had to teach the rebels how to honor authority, even when the one in authority wasn't worthy to be honored. The men wanted to kill Saul, but David wouldn't let them. He was showing them what it meant to have a true attitude of submission.

One day while Saul was chasing David in the wilderness of Engedi, David had an opportunity to kill Saul. Instead, he cut off a part of Saul's robe. He did this to prove to Saul that he had spared his life.

> David also arose afterward, and went out of the cave, and cried after Saul, saying, My lord the king. And when Saul looked behind him, David stooped with his face to the earth, and bowed himself. And David said to Saul, Wherefore hearest thou men's words, saying, Behold, David seeketh thy hurt? Behold, this day thine eyes have seen how that the LORD had delivered thee to day into mine hand in the cave: and some bade me kill thee: but mine eye spared thee; and I said, I will not put forth mine hand against my lord; for he is the LORD's anointed.
> —1 SAMUEL 24:8–10

David saw clearly that Saul was God's problem, not his problem. In spite of Saul's pitiful state and the fact that he was oppressed by demons, he was God's choice, and he had to be honored. The same is true for us today. Don't lay your hands on God's anointed! Don't gossip about them, or you are going to bring a curse to your life.

Whenever the Holy Spirit falls on someone or some church or some message, it's incredible. But just because a person is anointed and has experienced an element of success doesn't condone the bad character of the person or church that God happens to be using.

> For the gifts and calling of God are without repentance.
> —ROMANS 11:29

The glory is going to fall on someone who is using their gift and walking in the calling God gave them, but it doesn't mean they are mature. Therefore it should not surprise or disillusion you when great men and women of God do something that lacks integrity.

If your brother or sister in Christ is in trouble or error, you should pray for them and leave them to the Holy Spirit. Seek the grace David had to honor and recognize who has been used of God. Whether or not they are being used, you honor them. You don't have to invite them to dinner, but honor them if you are in their presence or when their name comes up in conversation.

Why is this so important? God chose them, and they are still His anointed until He takes them out. Even if their life and ministry are just flesh, materialism, hype, and gross manipulation now, they are still God's anointed.

> Moreover, my father, see, yea, see the skirt of thy robe in my hand: for in that I cut off the skirt of thy robe, and killed thee not, know thou and see that there is neither evil nor transgression in mine hand, and I have not sinned against thee; yet thou huntest my soul to take it.
>
> —1 SAMUEL 24:11

Did you notice that David addressed Saul as his father? But Saul is not David's father! Jesse is his father. Yet David acknowledges Saul as his spiritual father. He honored Saul even when he was full of demons, out of the will of God, cantankerous, rebellious, senile, and couldn't hear God if He showed up in a burning bush! He honored his spiritual authority even though his spiritual authority was out of the will of God.

> Children, obey your parents in the Lord: for this is right. Honour thy father and mother; which is the first commandment with promise; that it may be well with thee, and thou mayest live long on the earth.
>
> —EPHESIANS 6:1–3

In a spiritual sense, your spiritual authorities are your fathers and mothers. This says to me that we must honor any of the fathers and mothers of past movements of true Christianity. It's not righteous behavior to make fun of them or to vaunt ourselves up above them because we're being used today and they're not. We give them respect and we give them honor. I don't have to like them, but I have to honor them.

David told Saul that he could have killed him, but didn't. He let Saul know how it hurt him that Saul was trying to kill him. He said, "You're writing books about me; you're going around speaking evil about me; you're writing slanderous letters. You're dropping rumors all over the body of Christ trying to destroy me, but I haven't touched you."

> The LORD judge between me and thee, and the LORD avenge me of thee: but mine hand shall not be upon thee.
>
> —1 SAMUEL 24:12

67

In all the persecution from Saul, David remained strong. To the four hundred malcontents who followed him, he was an example of righteous submission. He taught them how to honor authority when authority was corrupt, and he showed the grace of God in action.

But Saul was not David's only test and trial. God then commanded David to go beyond the call of duty in meeting the needs of others, many times when David was in desperate need himself.

KEILAH: DOING ALL THINGS AS UNTO THE LORD

IN 1 SAMUEL, chapter 23, God told David to help the city of Keilah, which was being attacked by the Philistines. His men thought this was a great idea, because the spoils of war would meet their needs. However, David knew that Saul was trying to find out where he was in order to kill him. If he fought the Philistines in Keilah, Saul would know where he was. Nevertheless, David obeyed the Lord, fought, and won.

Then God told David to get out of town because Saul was coming. David asked the Lord if the men of Keilah, whom he had just delivered from the Philistines, would turn him in to Saul, and God said, "Yes."

Now, wouldn't you be just a little angry? David risked his life to save this stupid city, and now they're going to turn him in to Saul. To obey the Lord and meet the needs of the people of Keilah and of his own men, he put his life on the line, but they gave nothing to him in return.

Don't be surprised if a lot of people you help

don't prove to be faithful to you. They won't be! And you have to pass this test before you ever get to Zion. We must be faithful to meet the needs of others while we are in need ourselves, knowing that most of those we help are there for their own purposes, their own satisfaction, and there is no guarantee they will be faithful to us at all.

I read a story of a policeman who broke the window of a car in order to rescue a couple trapped inside. They were parked at "Lovers' Lane" and had become unconscious because of carbon monoxide fumes in the car. One month later the policeman received a bill for the broken window!

But the grace of God is for unworthy people like that couple. That's why *we* are saved! Salvation, which is by God's grace, is for unworthy people, and every human being is unworthy except Jesus Christ.

To be like Jesus, we have to be faithful to meet the needs of others *as unto the Lord,* not just to get something in return. Then God will cause us to be successful and to be vindicated if necessary.

As David served his people by obeying the voice of the Lord, God delivered him and his men out of the hands of Saul at every turn. One of the lessons of Adullam is that you can *never* expect fair treatment from the men and women you serve, but you can *always* expect the Lord to deliver and prosper you!

THE HARDEST LESSON

WE HAVE to learn to give ourselves to others while we ourselves have problems, and we have to help people who are not committed to our own personal welfare, our vision, or our church. They may never help us in return, they may never give a dime to us, yet we have to give all we have into their lives. This is a vital part of our development as saints of God.

There are a lot of people who come to church because it feeds their needs. These people will follow you or become your friend because you satisfy something in them. If you stop satisfying it because it's time for them to begin maturing and fending for themselves in a few areas, they may leave you. This is the toughest lesson of Adullam.

God wants to see His kingdom come, but some of us want our kingdom to come.

I'm committed to my congregation, good or bad. I'm there come hell or high water. No matter how many needs I have, I still have to help needy people, and so will you. No matter how many turn against me after I've poured my life into them, the grace that God extended to me must continue to be extended to others.

But how is it possible to lay down our lives as Jesus did, expecting nothing in return? Adullam represents the time when God anchors your heart in Jesus Christ and nothing else. Your identity and security are not in your friends, your job, whom you marry, what your children accomplish, how much money you have, where you live, or how you live. Whether you are a senior pastor, a worship leader, play an instrument, or lead a home group, you get your identity from Jesus.

The purpose of the experience at Adullam is to know that all your security is in Jesus. A lot of people who are in the ministry, even those who are very talented and anointed, are still terribly insecure. They get their identity from being on television, being famous, having lots of money, preaching a great message, and rubbing shoulders with other famous people who tell them how gifted they are.

Business professionals, athletes, and people in all walks of life can base their sense of importance and significance on their performance and on whom they know. The problem with basing your identity and security on these things is that when anything critical is said about you or any adversity comes your way, you crumble. Just like the man who built his house upon the sand, when the wind and rain come, you fall apart. (See Matthew 7:26–27.) You have no solid foundation under your life, ministry, or profession.

Knowing this, God desires to anchor us in no one but Himself, just as He did with David at Adullam. You get to Adullam because you have achieved a measure of success, and then every need and every problem hits your door! But as you immerse yourself in God to meet the needs of others, even when those you have come to love and count on turn against you, you can remain at peace. Getting to Adullam makes you a hero, but growing up at Adullam will make you secure.

HEBRON IS WHERE WE
LEARN TO **RELATE**
TO PEOPLE NOT ON
THE BASIS OF WHAT THEY
DO FOR US, BUT IN
RECOGNITION OF
GOD'S WORK IN BRINGING
US TOGETHER.

CHAPTER THREE

HEBRON: FAITHFUL IN RELATIONSHIPS

J ESUS SAID His church was going to be glorious, without spot and wrinkle. If the bride is going to be without spot and wrinkle, she must be washed and pressed! Have you felt pressed lately, like a hot steaming iron was rolling over you?

God has a way in which we are all matured, and it doesn't always feel good. Just like the little baby who has the legal rights to all of the benefits of the family, but gets it in bite-size pieces as he proves responsible, we are given our inheritance through a process of growth and development.

First, there's *Bethlehem,* where *we learn to be faithful in natural things.* When God brings us into the kingdom, we're told to do certain things to serve the body. Some of these tasks are not really exciting—straightening the chairs, cleaning up after people, or changing diapers. However, if we are faithful in them, we will be faithful in the greater and more weighty spiritual things.

Secondly, we come to *Adullam,* where *our anointing and success bring us a lot of problems.* Our success exposes the selfish ambition of jealous people and the fear of insecure people, brings the attack of the devil, brings tests, and tries all of our relationships. Because of our great victories, we attract all the needy people. However, in the midst of our own great neediness, we learn to meet the needs of others and find our security only in the Lord.

Now we come to *Hebron,* where *we commit ourselves to covenant relationships.* Back in Adullam, we gave ourselves to help people in order to get something in return. We were not really committed to their welfare. But when we get to Hebron, we commit ourselves to a relationship regardless of the circumstances, no matter how much it hurts.

COMFORT OR COVENANT?

WHEN THE romance and excitement of a new relationship has worn off and we begin to see flaws and faults, then we decide whether we are going on to Hebron or not. To pass the test of Hebron, we must stick together, fully committed, come hell or high water.

Where Adullam relationships are unstable, immature, and temporary, Hebron relationships are steady, mature, and last forever. Where Adullam relationships are based on need and selfish comfort, Hebron relationships are based on covenant and the grace of God, which always gives. The Adullam friend is a parasite, but the Hebron friend stands beside you in strength and unity no matter what happens.

Remember, it is perfectly all right to come to Adullam. All of us came to Jesus out of our need. I didn't come because I was such a great guy! I came out of my need, and He offered help. That's the baby stage, and it's a stage through which every believer goes. It's where we learn that God is for us and wants us to be whole human beings. "Jesus is my healer; Jesus is my deliverer; Jesus is my Savior. Oh, thank You, God, Jesus is my holy Band-Aid!"

But God expects us to go beyond the baby stage to a place where we come to Him recognizing we didn't choose Him; He chose us. We're called to serve Him. He's Lord; we're not. He expects us to come to sonship, where we realize, beyond the fact He is for us, we are for Him. We are created for His pleasure.

> Thou art worthy, O Lord, to receive glory and honour and power: for thou hast created all things, and for thy pleasure they are and were created.
> —REVELATION 4:11

Now we're beginning to wake up and realize what's going on! We're beginning to realize that Jesus doesn't want us to stay at Adullam. It is a temporary dwelling place He provided in order to bring us to a place of wholeness in Him.

As a minister, I have learned there are some people who love me and stay with me as long as the Holy Spirit is doing magnificent, marvelous things, but they are out the door the moment I have a dry spell and there doesn't seem to be any anointing. This is the Adullam crowd.

The Hebron crowd are the ones I'm looking for, because they will be with me and for me come rain or shine. When things are fantastic, they rejoice with me. When things are difficult, they pray for me. They understand the reality of the Christian life: Nobody's perfect, we all make mistakes, and even the greatest men and women of God go through times when they wonder if the Spirit of God has abandoned them.

Adullam is where my needs get met and I begin to put the Word of God to work in my life, where I'm discipled by those who are mature and led by those who know how to fight. But eventually I face the decision to go to Hebron, where I will begin to lay down my life for Jesus and for my brother and sister, choosing to walk in covenant love. Covenant love is loving someone to the death, loving them if it costs me everything.

A Change of Motive

In Matthew 4:23–25, we saw how Jesus was surrounded by an Adullam crowd. The disciples mistakenly assumed this crowd was Jesus' permanent crowd. They said, "Hey, we could build the kingdom out of this bunch!" Later on, they discovered this was not the case when Jesus declared to the multitudes:

> Verily, verily, I say unto you, Except ye eat the flesh of the Son of man, and drink his blood,

ye have no life in you. Whoso eateth my flesh,
and drinketh my blood, hath eternal life; and I
will raise him up at the last day.

—JOHN 6:53–54

Whoa! What is He talking about? What does He
mean when He says we have to eat His flesh and
drink His blood? In the passage of Scripture that follows Jesus proceeded to explain the covenant
relationship He was offering to mankind, but the
weight of His words was still too much for many of
His followers.

> This is that bread which came down from
> heaven: not as your fathers did eat manna,
> and are dead: he that eateth of this bread shall
> live for ever . . . It is the spirit that quickeneth;
> the flesh profiteth nothing: the words that I
> speak unto you, they are spirit, and they are
> life . . . From that time many of his disciples
> went back, and walked no more with him.
>
> —JOHN 6:58, 63, 66

What was Jesus doing? He was moving them from
the baby, immature, carnal relationship to one of
the heart and spirit. Not everybody made it.

It is often discouraging to see how many people
have been healed, delivered financially, have seen
angels, and worked miracles, but when the fire falls
they don't stick it out. They aren't around for Jesus
when times get tough. This is because miracles
don't produce character. Although we believe in
miracles, expect miracles, and often see them, they
will never make us strong in the Lord.

That's why you'll see all these flaky believers hanging around miracles who don't pay their bills, maintain a home, or pursue a relationship with their children. They are carnal, undisciplined, full of addictions, and held in bondage, because a miracle doesn't produce godly character.

Miracles are just a starting place where Jesus gets your attention, but if you don't go beyond that, you're finished. You won't fulfill your destiny. You'll make it to heaven—and may get there sooner than everybody else!—but you won't be an overcomer in this life.

Now this doesn't mean that people who fade into the woodwork can't come back! God's mercies are new every morning (Lam. 3:22–23). It just means if they do come back, they have to come back with a different motive.

Need-oriented Christianity will not keep you steady when Jesus turns around to you with a hard saying you cannot understand. It takes a little something extra to follow Jesus when He's not explaining what's going on!

When most of His followers left, Jesus asked the twelve, "Will ye also go away?" (John 6:67). The disciples did not know what was going on, and they had to reevaluate *why* they were following Him.

Between Adullam and Hebron there is a change of motive.

> And it came to pass after this, that David inquired of the LORD, saying, Shall I go up into any of the cities of Judah? And the LORD said unto him, Go up. And David said, Whither shall I go up? And he said, Unto Hebron. So

> David went up thither, and his two wives also, Ahinoam the Jezreelitess, and Abigail Nabal's wife the Carmelite. And his men that were with him did David bring up, every man with his household: and they dwelt in the cities of Hebron. And the men of Judah came, and there they anointed David king over the house of Judah. And they told David, saying, That the men of Jabeshgilead were they that buried Saul.
>
> —2 SAMUEL 2:1–4

Those who followed David to Hebron had a different motive than when they were at Adullam. Instead of coming to have their needs met, they came to anoint David king of Israel. Their relationship with David was no longer based on need, but on the realization that God had brought them together for a special reason.

When we recognize and understand how God moved sovereignly and/or miraculously in order for us to meet, we honor that relationship whether we get anything out of it or not. Why? Because the Holy Spirit must be accomplishing some big purpose!

Why did God bring you to your church? You better find out! If you don't *know* that He planted you where you are, you won't make it when the fire hits. You won't last, no matter how many shouts of "Praise the Lord" you utter.

I'm never impressed because you can prophesy. I'm not impressed because you can scream the loudest or dance the longest. I want to see if you can walk straight. Then I'll listen to your prophecy, and then I'll join you in the back flips!

Have you ever had God show you something about yourself that you didn't like? It didn't come when you were exercising a spiritual gift or as people fell down when you laid hands on them. It came when there was fire and testing and flood and rain—when everything was about to fall down. That's when you saw your Adullamish, carnal, selfish nature.

God tests our relationships and motives, not for *Him* to find out what's in us, but for *us* to find out what's in us. David wrote in Psalm 4:1, "Thou hast enlarged me when I was in distress." Are you going through distress? You're getting enlarged! And do you hate it? It's like getting a shot or eating vegetables you detest, but you do it because it's good for you. Nobody likes it, but it's necessary for you to grow up. Not many come through it, but if they do, Zion is a piece of cake!

Peter told Jesus that he would never deny Him. "I'm not really sure about the rest of the staff, but I do know me. I will be with you though all men forsake you."

Jesus replied, "Peter, the devil says you're all chaff, but I said you are not all chaff. You have a little reality in you. So I'm going to pray for you while the devil sifts you to expose the chaff. I believe that in the end you'll get rid of that evil stuff."

Things got worse for Peter after that. What was Jesus trying to accomplish? He knew Peter wasn't going to be any good to Him until he recognized that his motive for following Jesus was a carnal one, and thus repented and got his priorities straight.

Peter wanted to establish an earthly kingdom. He was trying to enhance his personal reputation and gain. He had come to Jesus out of need, out of what Jesus could do for him. He was not there because he saw that the true purpose for Jesus' coming into this world was to die on a cross.

After Peter denied Jesus three times, he realized how carnal his relationship with Jesus was. He swore, ran away, and wept bitterly. God had to expose that carnal motive in him. God showed Peter that it was time for him to move out of the cave at Adullam and begin to scale the cliffs of Hebron.

> Therefore judge nothing before the time, until the Lord come, who both will bring to light the hidden things of darkness, and will make manifest the counsels of the hearts: and then shall every man have praise of God.
> —1 CORINTHIANS 4:5

The secrets of all hearts will be made manifest, and that's not in heaven, that's now! The fire will come and show us what's in our hearts. It's discouraging to see what's in many hearts. You look at the lives of those who sing, usher, play instruments, are elders, or sit in the pew—and wonder if they heard a word of all the preaching.

They speak in tongues, they say *amen,* but their hearts are filled with lying, murmuring, deceit, and carnality. They lie, they run off at the first sign of trouble, they make excuses, and they blame you if you confront them.

God's not going to let anybody get away with

81

that stuff. They can flee to another church, but the fire will follow them. If they marry someone else, they will divorce again for the same reason. The problems are going to remain until they decide to grow up and overcome them God's way.

Watch these church hoppers. They keep hopping! Why? Because they're not dealing with the root of their trouble. The motivation of rebellion and carnality has not been destroyed. But God is going to see that it keeps coming up until they deal with it, or it will destroy their lives.

HEBRON: PLACE OF COVENANT

HEBRON IS twenty miles southeast of Jerusalem. It is located in a chain of mountains, the same chain in which Zion is found. However, it is higher than Zion. Zion is twenty-five hundred feet above sea level, and Hebron is three thousand feet above sea level.

Hebron is the highest city in earthly, natural Israel. Although Zion, the place of ruling and reigning, is our destination in the Christian life, Hebron is higher. If Zion is where we are going, why do we have to reach a higher place before we get there?

The name *Hebron* means "seat of association, being joined together, true fellowship." It is the burial place of the covenant fathers Abraham, Isaac, and Jacob. So we say Hebron means fellowship and covenant. This is a place where the rubber meets the road in relationships!

Since Hebron is the highest natural place in Israel, covenant making is the highest spiritual place you can come to in the body of Christ. There's nothing higher in the Christian life than the ability to make and keep a covenant. A life based on miracles, supernatural phenomenon, and Holy Ghost goosebumps will eventually fall, but a life based on covenant will stand.

Adullam was easy to get to because it was located in a valley, in a flat plain, so anybody could come through. It was easy to find. Spiritually speaking, in Adullam all you had to do was lift your hand, get baptized in the Holy Spirit, speak in tongues, prophesy, fall down, get healed, get delivered, get your needs met—you're in Adullam.

There's nothing for you to brag about because you were baptized in the Holy Spirit. Adullam is no big claim to fame! It's an easy place. But Hebron is a hard place to get to. It is out of the way, and in David's time there were no good roads. If you go to Hebron today, you will still not find a good road to get there. It is steep, rocky, and dangerous. Even in a car it is a lousy trip.

You have to go out of your way to get to Hebron. It is difficult, inaccessible, and you have to scale rocky, steep cliffs. That's all in the natural, but I hope you can hear the application in the spiritual. Keeping covenant relationships means pain!

Not everyone comes to Hebron, because it is hard to get there. Hebron is high ground, and it is inconvenient ground, so nobody would ever go there with an impure motive. If you come to Hebron, it is for one reason: God told you to go. It was the will of God for you to go there.

Because Hebron is the highest natural city, it represents the highest spiritual position you can come to in Christ. You don't come there by accident. You come there on purpose, committed to the Lord and His people, or you won't make it.

We come to Jesus, He meets our needs, but then He brings us to the place where we not only appreciate how He laid His life down for us, but we are now willing to lay our reputation and life down for Him and for our brothers and sisters—no matter what it costs.

Hebron is a place where you learn to fear God more than men. It is where you line your life up with His Word instead of the ever-changing opinions of men, put your money where your mouth is, and make yourself of no reputation.

When you come to Hebron, you come to make a covenant.

HIGHER GROUND MEANS HIGHER FAITH

MOST OF the church live at Adullam, where their faith is directed toward their own benefit. It's so much fun, and it feels so good. But you don't grow up in God because it feels good and your needs are getting met any more than you base your marriage on your feelings. Good feelings are the first to go in the fire!

Hebron is an act of your will, a choice to have more faith in God than you've ever had before. There's a faith that costs you everything you have. This faith is described in Hebrews 11, and the Bible gives us a list of saints who died in this kind of faith. It was a faith in something greater than their own lives.

God wants to bring you to a higher faith than you've ever known, where you relate to a person not because they bless you, but simply because they are a child of God. Jesus Christ died for them and, if necessary, you will die for them.

> Hereby perceive we the love of God, because he laid down his life for us: and we ought to lay down our lives for the brethren.
>
> —1 JOHN 3:16

This is the demonstration of what the Holy Spirit calls the love of God. Because Jesus laid His life down for us, we ought to lay down our lives for the brethren. This kind of love takes a great faith!

In America's government in Washington, DC, we have a standard of weights and measures. This standard insures that everybody in America who goes to any butcher shop or grocery store for a pound of meat gets sixteen ounces, not thirteen, and not seven. The government has guaranteed a pound to be sixteen ounces, and if the meat market doesn't meet that standard, they can be prosecuted.

Suppose you go to the grocery store, order a pound of steak, and the butcher gives you eight ounces. You say, "That's only eight ounces, and I ordered a pound."

The butcher says, "Well, you call it the way you see it, I call it the way I see it. It's close enough."

You say, "That's not close enough! It does not meet the standard that our government has set!"

God sets the standard of love in His Word, and His name is Jesus. Do you want the standard weight and measure of love, or do you want a deficient measure of love? What believers are giving each other in love could be compared to a butcher giving you an eight-ounce pound of meat.

God said the standard of love was laying down your life for your brother. When the body of Christ lives according to this standard, we won't ever have to worry about betrayal, evil speaking, gossip, slander, or murmuring. What's more, we can be confronted personally for sin or error (privately first, because you love me) and have the security that we won't be rejected and thrown out with the garbage just because we made a mistake.

Jesus is the measure, and this standard of love is the same in Great Britain, Zimbabwe, South Africa, Australia, and all over the world. This kingdom, the government of God that sets the standard, doesn't change in any nation on the earth. It's not what your preacher told you, not what your experience taught you, but what God says.

That doesn't mean we slobber on people when they're nice to us. It means we're nice to them even when they're ugly to us. It's not because they are worthy, but to honor Jesus who died for them.

We want God's forgiveness and love when we mess up, so when those with whom we are in covenant mess up, we had better be like Jesus and extend mercy. You say, "Well, he's offended me three times." Jesus said to forgive seventy times seven, so forgive him! Once every three minutes. When we see this in the church, we're going to see His glory on the body of Christ!

When God loves somebody, He loves at the cost of His own life. Convenient love says, "Well, I'll love you as long as I get to sing. I'll love you if I can be an elder. I'll love you as long as I'm getting some publicity. I'll love you if . . . " That's convenient love. You are a potential danger to others if you love this way, because you are unstable and immature. When the heat comes on, you're going to be deserting us in battle.

In order to meet the standard measure of love God has set, we must cleanse our hearts, get our motivations right, and move into a higher faith. A person who does this is someone you can count on, someone who understands a covenant, and someone you can have as a friend for life.

HIGHER GROUND MEANS HIGHER VISION

DAVID SPENT seven-and-a-half years in Hebron before he became king of Israel. He lived there all that time before the other ten tribes even accepted him as king. It was during this time that he had to learn to live in covenant.

He had to learn what it meant to commit himself to the will of God before God made him a ruler—so will I and so will you. If you are going to be a leader in the army of God, your word had better mean something! This isn't just for those who stand on the platform. Those who stand on the platform come from those who sit in the pews. Covenant is something God wants from all of His people.

As his men followed David, they discovered he was not just the answer to their financial problems, not just the one who was going to wipe out Saul and give them a new place in his kingdom. That's how they started, but that's not how they finished. They now saw David as God's anointed man with character, and what they saw changed them.

David was captain over the rebels, the malcontents,

the distressed, and those in debt. Though captain of the rebels, David was never rebellious. Though persecuted by corrupt authority, he maintained an attitude of submission to that authority.

David's character and conduct toward Saul changed those who followed him. His godly attitudes and behavior were displayed in front of rebellious men who didn't know the meaning of the word "character." However, in the end, they became like David.

> Then all Israel gathered themselves to David unto Hebron, saying, Behold, we are thy bone and thy flesh. And moreover in time past, even when Saul was king, thou wast he that leddest out and broughtest in Israel: and the Lord thy God said unto thee, Thou shalt feed my people Israel, and thou shalt be ruler over my people Israel. Therefore came all the elders of Israel to the king to Hebron; and David made a covenant with them in Hebron before the Lord; and they anointed David king over Israel, according to the word of the Lord by Samuel.
>
> —1 Chronicles 11:1–3

During the seven years David lived in Hebron, the men came to him; he didn't go to them. He didn't recruit; he didn't advertise; and he was not trying to make himself king. They came to Hebron and voluntarily made him their king.

Proverbs 18:16 says that a man's gift makes room for him. You don't make room for your gift, but your gift makes room for you. That's why I'm cautious of people who always advertise or promote their gift. Why do they do that? If they're still overwhelmed by their gift, they haven't learned that not only is God the giver of the gift, but He's the only One who makes room for the gift He gives. Promotion comes from the Lord.

If you are a self-made man, you'll be a self-destroyed man. But if you let God make you, nothing can cause you to fall. And it takes time! Don't be impatient. We want it now. I don't care if you can sing like a canary and make the angels appear. Wait until your character gets stable!

If one of our home group leaders is chomping at the bit to get a staff position and threatening to leave if they don't get it, I say, "Let them go!" I'm not going to promote anyone God hasn't told me to promote *when* He's told me to promote them. A person like that, who's more interested in "going up" than "growing up," is a dangerous threat to the well-being of our congregation.

It's when you aren't thinking about it all the time that you get the desire of your heart. When you are so sold-out to the Lord, laying down your life for the people, consumed with serving them and doing God's will for your life—that's when your dreams are realized. After all, God gave you those dreams! If you are faithful and walk in covenant, He's going to see they come to pass.

When David came to Hebron, he didn't tell his followers he was king; they recognized he was king. When they came to higher ground in the natural, they were coming to the higher vision of God's plan and purpose.

> And there came of the children of Benjamin and Judah to the hold unto David. And David went out to meet them, and answered and said unto them, If ye be come peaceably unto me to help me, mine heart shall be knit unto you: but if ye be come to betray me to mine enemies, seeing there is no wrong in mine hands, the God of our fathers look thereon, and rebuke it. Then the spirit came upon Amasai, who was chief of the captains, and he said, Thine are we, David, and on thy side, thou son of Jesse: peace, peace be unto thee, and peace be to thine helpers; for thy God helpeth thee. Then David received them, and made them captains of the band.
> —1 CHRONICLES 12:16–18

When these men came to David to volunteer, David didn't say, "Oh, thank God you're here! We need to build a crowd quickly. We've just opened this church and God's with me and I'm so glad to have anybody come." No! When all these men came to David, he challenged their commitment. He said, "Why are you here?"

Most of us would look at him and cry, "Well, you have some nerve! It looks like you need all the help you can get, Bud. You don't have anybody playing instruments, giving money, or parking the cars." But these men have climbed to higher ground because they have a higher vision than getting their needs met.

Also, David understood this principle: *You have to know that the motives of those you set in authority are right*. No matter what their gifting is, if they have come with an impure or an Adullam motive, later on they're going to cause you all kinds of problems.

> And we beseech you, brethren, to know them which labour among you, and are over you in the Lord, and admonish you.
> —1 THESSALONIANS 5:12

We can be so eager for people to be committed to us that we don't check them out and see if they're really committed to what God is accomplishing through us. We live in romantic idealism instead of honest reality.

But David comes right to the point. He wants to know if God has brought them there. Do they recognize what God is doing? Have they caught the vision? He's destined to rule a whole nation, and he's not playing games. If they came to betray him, he tells them God will judge them.

Still they said they wanted to follow him, because they believed David was God's choice as king. They knew David after the flesh at Adullam, but at Hebron they know him after the spirit. In 1 Chronicles 12:18 Amasai made a covenant commitment by the Holy Spirit, not the flesh.

Paul said he knew no man after the flesh (2 Cor. 5:16). There's a big difference in knowing somebody after the flesh and knowing them after the spirit. Fleshly relationships will not endure spiritual testings, which is why God allows the fire to fall. Carnal relationships will dissolve in the heat of a trial.

Joab is a good example. He joined David with a

selfish motive to be commander, and he betrayed him three times. Before David died he told Solomon to kill Joab because he had brought nothing but trouble during David's reign. But all the other mighty men came to David with hearts of servants, recognizing who David was in God. They had come to a higher vision than Adullam.

When he was in the cave, David didn't look like the anointed leader of Israel. He wasn't on the cover of *Charisma* magazine; he didn't have a tape-of-the-month ministry; he didn't have a program on TBN; but he was the king. For seventeen years he didn't have a crown on his head, but he was the man.

In every city there are churches with men God has appointed for a special purpose in the kingdom, but you won't recognize them in the flesh. They may not be the flashiest, most gifted, and noticeable in the natural. You'll only know these men and women after the spirit, not the flesh.

God won't allow them to get that "flash" early, because it will draw the wrong kind of people. They need people who are loyal to them. When they can't get out of the ditch, they stay together because God put them together, not because it is convenient or it's rewarding or they feel good. They may not feel good; they may wish they could kill one another; but they know God put them together and that's that.

HIGHER GROUND MEANS GREATER COMMITMENT

And Ruth said, Entreat me not to leave thee, or to return from following after thee: for whither thou goest, I will go; and where thou lodgest,

> I will lodge: thy people shall be my people,
> and thy God my God: where thou diest, will I
> die, and there will I be buried: the LORD do so
> to me, and more also, if ought but death part
> thee and me.
>
> —RUTH 1:16–17

This is covenant commitment, and it's rare. It's the way marriage should be. You know God brought you together to be married, so you stand against fleshly, emotional desires to strike or run or flee or divorce. If it kills you, you are going to give all you have to your spouse.

God commits to His people by the same standard. In the Bible every man He made a covenant with had a special place in His plan, and He did many things for them that He didn't do for other people. When He was going to destroy Sodom and Gomorrah, He said, "Oops, I can't do anything until I go talk to My friend Abraham."

On another occasion God told Moses He was going to destroy all the children of Israel and start over with just Moses. But Moses interceded for Israel, and God spared them. (In the next chapter, Moses begged God to kill them all, and God said He couldn't do it. If those two had ever agreed, there wouldn't be a Jew on the earth today!)

God commits Himself to people, and He commands us to commit ourselves to one another. If God does it, we should do it. The heart of covenant is that at the cost of your life you will keep your word. That's the highest point in spiritual experience. Ruling is only the result of that commitment.

Cindy and I cosigned three bank notes for three

Christian leaders. Not one of them paid the bank bill, and we had to pay every one of them off ourselves. We almost went bankrupt, but we paid them off. Why? Because my word is my bond, whether it's on paper or not.

My marriage certificate is not what holds me to Cindy, and a piece of paper won't hold you to your word either. It has to be an act of the will, a choice to do right no matter what the cost. It has nothing to do with feeling. Love is not an emotion; it is an act of your will. I don't love Cindy just because she does nice things for me. I choose to love her.

It's so easy to tell who on our staff has gone up to Hebron and who is still living in Adullam. When the church goes through a financial crises and we have to cut salaries, the ones who are in Hebron stay. The others will say, "Well, God called me up here, but we're going through some trouble now, so I feel it's the Lord's will that we leave."

Those who know they are here because God put them here will be faithful and stay put until the Lord tells them otherwise. They will persevere and stay in that place even if they have to do part-time work to support themselves.

God's love is a choice that results in action. He chose to love us and sent Jesus to die for us when we were still sinners (Rom. 5:8). Think about that! He just made up His mind to do it. Go look in the mirror. You're not worthy of it! Neither is anyone else.

When you have covenant character, you'll go farther than those with the greatest gifts who have no integrity. It means if you say you'll pay on Friday, it won't be on the next Monday. It will be Friday. And if the bank note is due on Friday and you can't pay it, you'll let the banker know on Thursday and try to work something out.

This way of living will pay you dividends in years to come and in eternity. We learned not to cosign on any more notes, but we kept covenant! We learned what David and his men learned at Hebron: The higher you go up, the greater your commitment must be, and your word is your bond.

THE PLACE OF RANKING

Hebron is the place of covenant, but it is also the place of ranking. Once covenant had been made, ranking could occur. David, like the Lord, ranked his men by their loyalty and achievement, not by their theology.

> These also are the chief of the mighty men whom David had, who strengthened themselves with him in his kingdom, and with all Israel, to make him king, according to the word of the LORD concerning Israel. And this is the number of the mighty men whom David had; Jashobeam, an Hachmonite, the chief of the captains: he lifted up his spear against three hundred slain by him at one time. And after him was Eleazar the son of Dodo, the Ahohite, who was one of the three mighties. He was with David at Pasdammim, and there the Philistines were gathered together to battle, where was a parcel of ground full of barley; and the people fled from before the Philistines. And they set themselves in the midst of that parcel, and delivered it, and slew

the Philistines; and the LORD saved them by a great deliverance. Now three of the thirty captains went down to the rock to David, into the cave of Adullam; and the host of the Philistines encamped in the valley of Rephaim. And David was then in the hold, and the Philistines' garrison was then at Bethlehem.
—1 CHRONICLES 11:10–16

David had the three, and he had the thirty; the three were over the thirty. Of the three, there was one chief. There was always a chief in a rank. Many Christians don't believe God can rank His people, but He does it anyway. The whole army of God is not all generals, sergeants, or privates. We are ranked in the kingdom of God.

Few of Jesus' followers had one-on-one contact with Him. He delegated authority to Peter, James, and John, then to the twelve, then to the seventy. That's the way God orders His kingdom. He delegates authority by ranking. If you got to one of the apostles, you got to Jesus.

When Paul couldn't go to somebody, he sent Timothy (Phil. 2:19–20). He said, "He has my heart, my vision, and when he comes, I come. He has the same spirit. He's my son, and I'm his father. It will be just like having me when he shows up."

Ranking doesn't mean somebody is better than somebody else; it means some are more responsible. Sometimes a thirteen-year-old child can be more mature and responsible than an eighteen-year-old. There are some eighteen-year-olds I wouldn't trust with my car, and yet there are thirteen-year-olds who can't drive that I would trust

96

explicitly if they could drive. They have proven their loyalty, character, maturity, and faithfulness; they are responsible.

In the kingdom of God, being older or having been around longer doesn't mean anything to God. He isn't going to give you the keys to the car on Friday night, because He knows you'll break curfew and might not come home, even though you're thirty years old. To others, who may not have been saved as long as you have, He may turn around and give them the car. He knows they are responsible enough to handle it and do what He wants done with it.

Jesus is no respecter of persons, but Jesus had the three, and the twelve, and the seventy. Was there a ranking? Yes! And the one He loved best was John the Beloved. To whom did He give His mother? John. He didn't give her to the seventy. Why? John was the one with whom Jesus could entrust the most. He was the most responsible.

Ranking is not determined by gifting or theology, but by your loyalty and achievement—not fleshly achievement, but spiritual maturity.

We, on the other hand, rank by theology. "Well, what do you believe about the Second Coming? What do you believe about dancing? What do you believe about women wearing pants? What do you believe about speaking in tongues?" God doesn't rank that way!

Many Christians are upset because God is granting authority to some men and women who don't adhere to their strict doctrinal beliefs. It shakes them up that He ranks some people with different doctrinal beliefs ahead of those with whom they agree.

David did it God's way. He ranked by loyalty and achievement. For example, one day after a hard battle with the Philistines, he was in the cave reminiscing. He was not giving orders when he said, "Boy, I sure wish I had a drink of that cold water from the well in Bethlehem." This is not a command. David was just talking to himself. But the three who were later placed over the thirty overheard him.

A few hours went by, a cloud of dust rolled in from nowhere, and David turned around to see these three guys with blood all over them, sweat pouring down, and their swords in their hands. As the three of them grinned from ear to ear, one of them held up a canteen of water and said, "Have a drink, David."

David asked them where they got the water, and they laughed, "We got it at the well of Bethlehem."

"Bethlehem? You guys had to kill some Philistines!"

"Yeah, we took out a whole battalion!"

David said, "I can't drink this water. It is too precious." He poured it out as an offering unto the Lord because it was too great a sacrifice. What that tells me is this: They served David as unto the Lord, and David received it as unto the Lord.

Do you understand why these three were the closest to David? They were 100 percent dedicated to their king and totally committed to laying their lives down for him in both the smallest and greatest of battles.

We're not supposed to be impressed by theology or gifting, but by loyalty and achievement. Hebron is a place where it's not what we believe that ranks us, but whether we are faithful to the covenant and obedient to the command.

WHEN COVENANT IS ESTABLISHED, GOD CAN BRING THE INCREASE

> For at that time day by day there came to David to help him, until it was a great host, like the host of God.
>
> —1 CHRONICLES 12:22

There are three things we need to understand from this scripture. First, *the growth rate was day by day*. Second, *men came to David. David didn't go get the men*. Third, *their motive was to help David*. They came to David at Adullam to get David's help, but in Hebron they came to help David at the expense of their lives. Their motive has changed. This is much more costly, and the result was a great army like the army of God.

> And they, continuing daily with one accord in the temple, and breaking bread from house to house, did eat their meat with gladness and singleness of heart, praising God, and having favour with all the people. And the Lord added to the church daily such as should be saved.
>
> —ACTS 2:46–47

These principles are keys for us today. If we are going to see revival as recorded in the Book of Acts, we are going to have to trust God to add to the church day by day. We don't have to strive and sweat to build our churches; we just have to be faithful in the natural things, faithful when we are in need, and faithful in relationships. Then God will bring the people in at the right time.

> And of the children of Ephraim twenty thousand and eight hundred, mighty men of valor, famous throughout the house of their fathers. And of the half tribe of Manasseh eighteen thousand, which were expressed by name, to come and make David king. And of the children of Issachar, which were men that had understanding of the times, to know what Israel ought to do; the heads of them were two hundred; and all their brethren were at their commandment. Of Zebulun, such as went forth to battle, expert in war, with all instruments of war, fifty thousand, which could keep rank: they were not of double heart.
>
> —1 CHRONICLES 12:30–33

God always had these great men, but now He adds them to David because a covenant is made. Now there is trust, a commitment of loyalty, and God can begin bringing in the hardware. He can add to a place where He finds fellowship that is founded on covenant.

God often withholds provision until the selfish carnality is exposed and purged and men are in covenant relationship. He has everything we need, but He's waiting for a greater commitment. He has loads of musicians, singers, and leaders. He has wisdom and money, but He waits to see when He can add it. He doesn't want to waste it. He wants to add it when we come into covenant, when He knows He can trust us with it.

DON'T DESPISE SMALL BEGINNINGS

HEBRON IS a place where small beginnings grow into greatness. You recognize that God put you in the nursery to change diapers. As you are faithful, you meet some people who become covenant friends. One day they introduce you to the head of Sunday school, and the Lord tells that person you are to teach a class. Suddenly one of your dreams is realized, and you have been sovereignly placed in a position of authority.

Think what you would have lost had you refused to change diapers! The people who complain the most won't start small, and they despise small beginnings. They are the ones who want a personal audience with the pastor whenever they feel like talking to him. However, that isn't possible in a five-thousand-member congregation, and it wasn't possible in Jesus' time either.

If you're called to pastor, get in a home group. When you're faithful in the home group, then God will promote you to pastor the home group. He will start you with something you can handle, not a five-thousand-member congregation. The home group is where you can be discipled, nurtured, prove faithful in natural things, and then promoted.

Then God will bring you the needy people. If you're faithful with needy people while you yourself have needs, He'll bring you to Hebron in a covenant commitment. And that's where your small beginning explodes into a mighty move of God in and through your life.

When we get to the place of covenant, there will be no more jealousy, no more selfish ambition, no more striving, no more contention, and no more murmuring. Doing right will not be based on advantage, but "I'll die, but I'll do it right." We will go all the way to the place of death to do the will of God. And when we begin to operate on that high level of commitment and covenant toward God and toward others, He can place us in a position of rulership.

**JESUS CHRIST IS GLORIFIED
WHEN WE LEARN
TO LIVE AS HE LIVED,
REIGNING WITH
HIM IN LIFE.**

CHAPTER FOUR

ZION: FAITHFUL
IN RULING

UNTIL DAVID and his mighty men stormed Zion, no man of God had ever taken it. Joshua didn't do it; the judges didn't do it;Saul didn't do it—none of them did it. That is why, when David and his men marched on Zion, the Jebusites who occupied it taunted them with, "You're not going to get up here, David, because nobody else before has ever kicked us out."

Nobody had been able to occupy Zion; it was a natural, impenetrable fortress. However, Hebron was higher than Zion, steeper than Zion, rockier than Zion, and more inaccessible than Zion; and David and his men had conquered it. They had been in the most hellacious place for seven years and had subdued it, so Zion looked easy compared to where they had been! David's army destroyed the Jebusites in a day.

This shows us that we can pull down strongholds in our lives and demonic fortifications over our cities that have been impossible to crack in the past—*if* we can conquer Hebron, the place of covenant relationships. Our greatest enemies are not demons of cancer or abortion, but the demons of disunity, disloyalty, and selfish carnality. When these things die, everything else in the kingdom of darkness will begin to come down.

The mighty men came to Hebron with different motives, and through their experience there, as they formed covenant relationships, they were prepared for Zion. It's impossible to go from Adullam to Zion, because if you're camping out in the cave of Adullam, you don't see the big picture. All you can see is yourself and what you want; you don't see what God is doing. In that level of maturity, you'll never be able to take Zion. To take Zion, the body of Christ must come into covenant relationships. Then God shares rulership with His people.

The trouble is, we get religious instead of faithful. And that disqualifies us. We think we qualify because we're a prophetess or an apostle or we glow in the dark or have three angels that follow us. But God is watching to see if we pay our bills, cut our grass, treat our spouses nice, train up our children in the way they should go, and walk in covenant, keeping our word to the death.

Zion is a natural by-product of having been faithful in the natural things, faithful to meet the needs of others while you are in need, and faithful in covenant relationships. Zion also speaks of being faithful in reigning, and it represents a corporate victory, not an individual victory.

Don't Go Alone

THERE ARE some areas of your life in which you will never reign alone. Let's face it; there are times when it feels like the devil is trying to absolutely take you out, and having a strong covenant brother or sister to stand by you makes the crucial difference.

This is why we're hearing so much about team ministry, working in covenant together, and protecting one another. Sometimes I don't want to be alone against the enemy. You can feel outnumbered, no matter how Charismatic you are! The devil can be an able match for any one of us, because it is always harder to fight a battle by yourself.

> Who passing through the valley of Baca [weeping] make it a well; the rain also filleth the pools. They go from strength to strength, every one of them in Zion appeareth before God.
>
> —PSALM 84:6–7

Those who go through times of trouble and weeping, discovering life and strength, are the ones who will get to Zion. They've been through the fire, come through it successfully, and are proven warriors. And whatever they've accomplished, big or small, they know they owe a great measure of their success to faithful men and women who helped them. They wouldn't have made it if their covenant brothers and sisters hadn't been there.

I can look back and see strategic people, men and women whom God placed in my life to help me make it. My advice to anyone who desires to reign in life would be: Don't try to do it alone. You need others. You need other believers to pray for your safety, for your maturity, and for God to deliver you from deception or bad relationships.

David was a faithful ruler, a faithful governor, and a faithful overseer. However, without the mighty men he could not have taken Zion. The Holy Spirit is telling us we are not "lone rangers" in the Christian life. We can only do so much by ourselves. Eventually, to fulfill our destiny and do the will of God for our lives, we are going to need to come into covenant with other believers.

Don't Be Premature

WHENEVER THE subject of ruling and reigning comes up, and you think about everything that God has put in your heart—the dreams which are burning to be accomplished right now—you will be tempted to rush the whole process. However, as we have seen before, God is more interested in the production of character than the provision of comfort.

We want comfort right now; God wants character, which takes time. To get character out of my children I may have to make them uncomfortable, and we are no different. God doesn't mind upsetting our plans if it produces character in us. (This isn't shouting material, but it will keep your heart steadfast when the flood comes to overwhelm you!)

When God promotes us, we're always ready, but when we promote ourselves, it is always premature. You can have a destiny or an inheritance and get it too soon and lose it. The prodigal son had an inheritance, but he took it prematurely and wasted it. He was restored to sonship, but he didn't get another inheritance. Don't go off half-cocked and blow your inheritance!

We know that a premature baby is a baby who is born too soon. Many babies are lost because they come into the world prematurely. Likewise, if you promote yourself, you can come into a position before the fullness of time God has set for it. Like a premature baby in the natural, you can be very weak, inept, and can even die.

It isn't because God doesn't want to promote you. He put that desire in you in the first place. But you can get there too soon by not listening to the Holy Spirit and trusting Him to lead you into it at the right time. This is what the Bible calls patience and faith, working together to see the promises of God fulfilled in your life. (See Hebrews 6:12.)

Spirituality is aggressive in obedience, but not pushy. Individuals who are carnal always promote themselves. Push, push, push! They think too highly of themselves, and they are going to crash and burn one day if they don't wake up to the fact that only God can promote them.

Jesus said that if you exalt yourself, you are going to be humiliated, but if you humble yourself, you will be exalted. (See Matthew 23:1–12.) If you come to a meeting, you should take the back seat and let the pastor ask you to come to the front seat. If you take the front seat, the pastor might stand you up in front of everybody and march you to the back. What a terrible experience! In front of God and everybody you're being taken to the back!

When I get into a car with other ministers I always go for the back seat. They have to kill me to get me in the front seat. That's a principle that will keep you safe! You take the last piece of pie, you serve everyone before you get yours, and you don't take the first in anything. It's a lifestyle that will keep you humble.

When people promote themselves they don't show up with the grace of God, and so they don't have the ability to function properly. Then God has to put them in a back seat, and that's totally humiliating. Now if they can learn from it, praise God! But wouldn't it be better to have faith and patience and trust God to promote you in the first place?

God always gives you a promotion right on time, exactly when you are ready. Isn't that good? I thank God for His wisdom, because sometimes I think I'm ready and I'm not. I've learned to trust His judgment and rest in it! He won't keep me back one day too long; He won't promote me one day too soon.

If I'm impatient and think my circumstances are not fair, I balance that out by knowing God's character. He's perfectly just, perfectly righteous, and He treats everyone the same. He made me; He knows what He has for me; and He knows when I'm ready to receive it. I never have to worry about if and when it is going to come; I just have to do what He's asked me to do. This is resting in the Lord.

When God puts you in a position of authority, He will also have seen to it that you have been well prepared. God didn't give Zion to David until he was ready for it. The only reason Zion was so easy to take was because David and his men had passed the tests of Bethlehem, Adullam, and Hebron.

We are talking about Zion, so let's take this concept to the corporate level. The church has often promoted itself beyond its ability to produce, and we've been humiliated in the eyes of the world many times. We've boasted and bragged, made declarations, and come up short. We haven't understood that our job is not to promote ourselves in the world, but to be faithful in the natural things, in need, and in relationships. Then God will do the promoting.

God's business is to add people to us as we are ready, but our advertising exceeds our production. We could be sued for false advertising! How about those slogans that show up on Sunday: "Where miracles happen every day." Then, in two years they are bankrupt and the building is for lease! Would you say that's false advertising?

How about this: "The friendliest church in town." Of the five hundred churches in your city, you are the friendliest one? Then there's a church split, and the new church is called Fellowship Church. What garbage! How about those who call themselves Revival Church. Where's the revival? We are promoting, and God's looking for production.

I would never use those names until it's an actual fact, because if it's an actual fact, then God has brought it to pass. If it's an actual fact, then we aren't just whistling in the dark wishing we were something we are not. And we don't have to advertise, because God has a way of getting the word out about something He's doing.

When we put ourselves in the front seat, the Lord says, "Excuse Me, church, come to the back seat; you're not ready to rule. You haven't even been to Hebron yet. You have just committed to Me out of what I can do for you, not for what you can do for

Me. And you've committed to each other out of selfish carnality and need, not because you see what I'm doing in your lives."

You're not ready to reign until you're willing to give your life for Jesus—your whole life. Now that's a big step! Are you willing to give your career, your reputation, rights, joy, privileges, happiness, well-being, security, and finances for Jesus? Furthermore, are you willing to do the same for your brother or sister in Christ?

This is corporate covenant, and we won't take Zion until that happens. God will never bring the church to Zion as a premature baby, divided and strife-ridden. She will be a grown-up, spotless Bride, who walks in covenant and love.

Take It All

> And David and all Israel went to Jerusalem, which is Jebus; where the Jebusites were, the inhabitants of the land. And the inhabitants of Jebus said to David, Thou shalt not come hither. Nevertheless David took the castle of Zion, which is the city of David. And David said, Whosoever smiteth the Jebusites first shall be chief and captain. So Joab the son of Zeruiah went first up, and was chief. And David dwelt in the castle; therefore they called it the city of David. And he built the city round about, even from Millo round about: and Joab repaired the rest of the city. So David waxed greater and greater: for the Lord of hosts was with him.
>
> —1 Chronicles 11:4–9

111

Before David took Zion, Jerusalem did not exist. It was called Jebus, because it was inhabited by the Jebusites. As a natural fortress on a mountain, surrounded by mountains, Zion had only one way into it. From a military standpoint it was practically impregnable. There was no way to conquer it.

It's amazing that Joshua, with all his conquests in the Promised Land, never took out the Jebusites. Gideon and all of the judges never defeated them. From the time of Israel's entrance into the land and the possession of the borders of all the land that God promised, the Israelites still never overcame them—until David and his mighty men came on the scene.

For years and years this stronghold against the Lord had existed, and not until the army of Israel was united under David would it be taken down. In the same way there are spiritual strongholds that the church has never been able to bring down. There are strongholds in our personal lives and demonic fortifications over our cities that have not yet come under the rule of God. Churches have come and churches have gone, and still these enemies remain.

God intends that we occupy *everything* He's assigned to us, not *some* of it. He wants us to possess all He has given to us. Therefore, we don't want a partial-victory mentality. A partial-victory mentality says, "Well, I'm better than I've ever been before, and I have more than most people." But that's not what God has for you!

I want everything I have coming to me legally in Christ. I don't want three-fourths of it, but all of it. Likewise the church needs to rise up with a total-victory mentality, which is what Zion represents spiritually.

A partial-victory mentality is also a partial-obedience mentality. It's really disobeying the Word of God by trying to find loopholes, and the Bible calls that sin. A great example of this is found in 1 Samuel, chapter 15. Saul returned from battle and told Samuel he had obeyed the commandment of the Lord when he really had not.

The Lord had commanded Saul to kill every Amalekite, including the women and children, as well as every animal they owned. In other words, He didn't want a trace of the Amalekite civilization to be found when Saul was finished with them.

When Saul returned from the battle and boasted about the great job he had done, Samuel asked him, "How come I'm hearing these oxen and sheep bleating in my ears?" It was obvious Saul had not totally obeyed the Lord. What he had not destroyed was the best of the Amalekites. He had not killed the king or the finest livestock.

You see, Saul had turned from the direct and simple commandment of the Lord to his own feeble and stupid understanding. He thought, *Hey, let's parade this king through the streets of our cities and show how great we are, and, what's more, we'll take the best of their livestock and sacrifice them to the Lord!*

The Amalekites represent the flesh, and God won't accept even the best flesh. He doesn't want any of it! What He wants is a people who will obey His Word and follow the leading of His Spirit. This is Samuel's reply to Saul.

> And Samuel said, Hath the LORD as great
> delight in burnt offerings and sacrifices, as in
> obeying the voice of the LORD? Behold, to
> obey is better than sacrifice, and to hearken
> than the fat of rams. For rebellion is as the sin
> of witchcraft, and stubbornness is as iniquity
> and idolatry. Because thou hast rejected the
> word of the LORD, he hath also rejected thee
> from being king.
> —1 SAMUEL 15:22–23

Saul was rejected because he disobeyed the Lord and offered Him flesh. Often in the Old Testament, when a king did what was right in the sight of God, the Bible follows the account of his reign with the statement that still the "high places" were not taken down. (See 1 Kings 15:14; 22:43; 2 Chronicles 20:33.) For Old Testament Israel the high places were pagan altars at the top of mountains, but for the church they are spiritual fortresses over our cities and strongholds in our personal lives.

> For we wrestle not against flesh and blood,
> but against principalities, against powers,
> against the rulers of darkness of this world,
> against spiritual wickedness in high places.
> —EPHESIANS 6:12

There have been some conquests and some measure of victory for the church, but then Saul had some measure of victory over the Amalekites also. The church has yet to fully obey the Word of God, which says that every enemy must be put under the feet of Jesus.

There are spiritual fortifications that have held out against the people of God. Why? Because it isn't the glitz and the glamour and the miracles and spiritual gifts that are going to bring them down. The Adullam crowd fell under the power of God, raised the dead, and saw signs and wonders, but they didn't establish the kingdom because they weren't walking in covenant.

When the heat was on and Jesus had been arrested, even the best of His followers, the apostles, said they never knew Him. These guys walked with Him, saw Him walk on water and heal the sick, and He even paid their taxes. Yet in the moment of Jesus' need they denied Him. That's why you cannot take down the principalities and powers of darkness when you are camped in Adullam. The church has got to come to Hebron before these high places are going to fall.

A lot of lone rangers have run off and attempted to pull down the strongholds that are still there, and some of these self-appointed leaders don't even exist anymore. What's more, the Jebusites are still there. Something has to happen to the people of God that will prepare us to come against these evil spiritual fortifications over our lives, homes, local churches, cities, and nations.

We should not wait for anything or anybody to adopt a victorious mentality. If we don't have a victorious mentality right now, we are in unbelief and sin! If we don't believe we can reign in life through Jesus Christ, overcoming humanism, liberalism, communism, or any other -ism, we had better leave the Jebusites alone!

We have to have total victory, nothing less.

Satan's not out just to hurt us; he's out to destroy us. He is not going to compromise with us, and there's no reason we should compromise with him. He will steal, kill, and destroy. That has to be our mindset against the devil. We're not out to get a piece of the action; we're out to see the devil come down. Not a little bit of victory, but complete victory!

UNITY COMMANDS BLESSING

THE DEVIL defeats us by keeping us separated and divided. He puts breaches in our relationships by getting us all upset about things that don't really matter.

We are told in Matthew 18:19, "Again I say unto you, That if two of you shall agree on earth as touching anything that they shall ask, it shall be done for them of my Father which is in heaven." That's the place of agreement; that's the place of victory for the church.

> Behold, how good and how pleasant it is for brethren to dwell together in unity! It is like the precious ointment upon the head, that ran down the beard, even Aaron's beard: that went down to the skirts of his garments; as the dew of Hermon, and as the dew that descended upon the mountains of Zion: for there the LORD commanded the blessing, even life for ever-more.
>
> —PSALM 133:1–3

How would you like to walk around in a position in God where He is commanding blessing? How would you like to be the devil trying to mess with someone over whom God Himself commands blessings to come? If God's people come together in covenant unity, there is no way the devil can cause division and defeat us.

If you can stretch yourself a little bit, you will see how we can literally be a church upon which God commands blessing. The key is *unity*. If you walk in unity, you can have a home upon which God commands blessing, a ministry where you walk around blessed even if nobody else is, and your church can be a harmonious beacon of light to your city. You can leave the devil scratching his head, wondering what is happening.

The alternative is to stay in Adullam, getting what you can, with no regard for what God wants to do, making no attempt to get along with anyone else— unless, of course, there's something in it for you. But God won't listen to you as long as you disagree and have discord with one another. And then you wonder why you aren't going anywhere!

Remember, the devil wants to be your Holy Spirit. He mimics the Holy Spirit in a voice you under-stand. If you're Pentecostal, he speaks in Pentecostal language, and he tells you not to talk to Baptists. If you're Hispanic, he speaks in your Hispanic tongue and says, "Stay away from those other ethnic groups over there."

Satan never says, "Hey, this is the devil, and I have a good idea for you." He comes through your personality, your vocabulary, your race, your reli-gious notions, and uses all your familiar terms to separate you from your brothers and sisters and cause strife and division.

It takes discernment to locate the devil's devices, and discernment comes when you and your brother are walking arm in arm in the power of the Holy Ghost with the Word hid in your hearts. The Bible warns us again and again not to be deceived. We need covenant brothers and sisters to go after principalities with us. We can't go alone, or we'll get killed.

Zion is corporate; it is not individual. All the men who came to David were in one accord and were skilled in war. They kept rank and had the heart to make David king. These were men who were walking in powerful unity and vast experience. They all knew what to do. They knew how to do it well, and they knew why they were doing it. After Hebron they understood and practiced unity; taking Zion was like a trip to Disneyland!

FRIENDLY FIRE

IN THE heat of battle my life often depends on whether the guy next to me knows how to stay in rank and keep his focus on what God is doing. If he gets out of place, if he breaks rank, or if he's distracted, I could be seriously wounded or even killed by the enemy. Even worse, if he gets deceived by the enemy and thinks I'm his enemy, he could turn around and shoot me himself!

In the military they call that friendly fire. There's nothing friendly about it! It means your own guys shot you by accident. The body of Christ, under the influence, is experiencing a lot of friendly fire these days! We're going around shooting our brothers and sisters instead of standing in unity and taking the enemy out, fighting together regardless of differences in theology.

Rather than take on the devil we take on each other. One denomination takes on another denomination. One movement takes on another movement. In reality, there's only one central doctrine in the body of Christ: Jesus Christ and Him crucified. After that's established, we join together for the Great Commission.

If you believe Jesus is the resurrected Son of God and you've made Him your Lord and Savior, let's march into war together! I don't care if you're Charismatic or evangelical, Catholic or Pentecostal, pre-trib, mid-trib, or post-trib. If you are committed to Jesus Christ, I'm totally committed to you.

These are the mighty men in today's church—men who won't break rank, won't lose the objective of God, and who are committed to each other. You can count on them whether they feel good or not.

UNITY INTIMIDATES THE ENEMY

WHEN DAVID came to Jebus the Jebusites were quick to let him know that no Israelite had ever been able to take the fortress of Zion. And that's what the devil says to you. "You're just like all the rest. Nobody's ever taken me down, and you won't either. No one in your family has ever been able to overcome this, and they were Christians, too. What makes you think you can?"

Satan intimidates whole churches as well as individual Christians, but there's something terrifying to the enemy when he sees a bunch of powerful men walking in covenant unity. Military leaders understand that power and make their soldiers break rank as they cross a bridge. You see, if they walk in order, it sets up a rhythm that can shake a bridge and break it. We're talking about a formidable, mighty force, the sight and sound of which can cause the enemy to shake in their shoes!

If that is true in the natural realm, it must be true in the spiritual realm. Anyone who opposes the cause of Christ is terrified when they see men and women in the church walking in unity. I don't believe we realize just how awesome a sight that is to our enemy, because if we did we'd start getting our act together.

Jesus has already defeated the devil. We know He made a show of all the demonic principalities and powers openly (Col. 2:15). Why then, if Satan and his army have been conquered, don't we come together and put him under the feet of the body of Christ?

God put our feet on Satan's neck, and He wants to see the reality of it in our daily lives. But in order to get there, we must recognize and put into practice His strategy for victory.

GOD'S WINNING STRATEGY

WHEN THE Jebusites saw David's army coming they began to mock him, telling him he wouldn't be any different from the rest who had tried and failed to conquer them in the past. "You can't come up here, David. You won't make it. Even our crippled men will be able to keep you out." You know what David did? He didn't go up there. David took Jebus by *delegated authority.*

And the king and his men went to Jerusalem unto the Jebusites, the inhabitants of the land: which spake unto David, saying, Except thou take away the blind and the lame, thou shalt not come in hither: thinking, David cannot come in hither. Nevertheless David took the strong hold of Zion: the same is the city of David. And David said on that day, Whosoever getteth up to the gutter, and smiteth the Jebusites, and the lame and the blind, that are hated of David's soul, he shall be chief and captain. Wherefore they said, The blind and the lame shall not come into the house. So David dwelt in the fort, and called it the city of David. And David built round about from Millo and inward. And David went on, and grew great, and the LORD God of hosts was with him.

—2 SAMUEL 5:6–10

David said, "Boys, the first one of you who kills a Jebusite will be captain of the army." These men didn't line up in single file and wonder which guy was going to get lucky. They charged up the mountain like a unified mob of wild men, crying, "Let me have one!" The Jebusites had never been hit with a crowd like that before!

David released thousands of screaming and hollering men who had already scaled the cliffs of Hebron, which was much more difficult than Zion. After seven years of Hebron, their lungs could take the thin air. They were all in great shape. From their standpoint Zion was an easy conquest, and they took it in a day. David went up after they had completely subdued it and called it the city of David.

When David destroyed the Jebusites and established the government of Israel on Mount Zion, it was a type and shadow of Jesus Christ spoiling principalities and powers and establishing the kingdom of God, or the government of God, on the earth. (See Colossians 2:15.)

> And what is the exceeding greatness of his power to us-ward who believe, according to the working of his mighty power, which he wrought in Christ, when he raised him from the dead, and set him at his own right hand in the heavenly places, far above all principality, and power, and might, and dominion, and every name that is named, not only in this world, but also in that which is to come: and hath put all things under his feet, and gave him to be the head over all things to the church, which is his body, the fulness of him that filleth all in all.
>
> —EPHESIANS 1:19–23

Just as David took Zion through delegated authority, the Father destroyed all the works of the enemy by the delegated authority given to His Son, Jesus Christ. Then Jesus turned around to the church and said, " . . . as my Father hath sent me, even so send I you." As the Father delegated His authority to Jesus, Jesus delegates His authority to His body. Jesus has knocked a hole in the heavenlies so you and I can go through and follow Him into spiritual victory!

This Jesus hath God raised up, whereof we all are witnesses. Therefore being by the right hand of God exalted, and having received of the Father the promise of the Holy Ghost, he hath shed forth this, which ye now see and hear. For David is not ascended into the heavens: but he saith himself, The LORD said unto my Lord, Sit thou on my right hand, until I make thy foes thy footstool.

—ACTS 2:32–35

Peter is preaching on the day of Pentecost, and he's quoting Psalm 110:1. The disciples knew that Jesus had sat down at the right hand of the Father because He had sent the Holy Spirit. The Father told Jesus to sit at His right hand until all the enemies of Jesus Christ are subdued under His feet, and the feet are on the body, the church. (Jesus also quotes Psalm 110:1 in Matthew 22:44, and the same verse is paraphrased in 1 Corinthians 15:25 and Hebrews 1:13.)

I don't believe we can conquer anything without the headship of Jesus Christ. You cannot exalt the body above the head, and the body is so intimately related to the head that the will of the head is manifested through the body. This is true in your natural body, and it is true in the body of Christ.

Jesus is the head of the church; we are His body; and when we are rightly related to Jesus in covenant, His will can be done in the earth. The will of God is accomplished through a body that is properly related to Him. A lot of Christians believe Jesus ought to do everything, but the Bible says that Jesus has already done all He's going to do in the realm of taking authority. He has already spoiled principalities and powers and destroyed the devil (Heb. 2:14).

Jesus legally and totally defeated Satan and his army of demons. All authority was given to Him in heaven and earth (Matt. 28:18). Then He delegated His authority to us and commissioned us to go do His work on the earth. Just as it was glorious for David to say to his men, "Go get them!" and see that impenetrable fortress fall, how much more glorious for the Lord to cry, "Go get them!" and watch the enemy of the ages come down!

MAKING DISCIPLES

GOD'S WINNING strategy won't be effective if you haven't taken the time to train and prepare those to whom you delegate authority. David's mighty men were able to take Zion because David had seen to it that the qualities of character and skill present in his own life were reproduced in those who followed him.

Likewise Jesus is building His church to be like Him. The body of Christ must be conformed to the thinking and behavior of the Head. In the knowledge of Jesus' victory, in the authority and power of His name, we are to go and teach all nations, preaching the gospel to every creature (Matt. 28:19–20; Mark 16:15). This is another way of saying, "Go make disciples."

As we study the Word and then go out and do it, as we line our lives up with Scripture, follow the leading of the Holy Spirit, and lay down our lives for God and each other, we are being changed to be like Jesus (2 Cor. 3:18). When we grow up in Him, we will be able to do what He did: Make disciples.

The mark of a great leader is that he reproduces himself. David's mighty men were inspired by David in the same way the church is empowered by Jesus to become mature in wisdom and character. Something is wrong if you have been born again for years and are not seeing any victory and progress in your life.

There are those who hang around church for years and still remain big jerks; their feelings are easily hurt; they always feel rejected and offended; and we have to treat them like a baby. They've missed the whole point of Christianity!

We're supposed to be ruling and reigning with Him, not sucking the bottle and having our diapers changed when we're thirty-five years old! The sad thing is that many believers live this way and think it's normal. They avoid growing up, and some even go so far as to believe that thinking, talking, and acting like Jesus is heresy.

> For whom he did foreknow, he also did predestinate to be conformed to the image of his Son, that he might be the firstborn among many brethren.
>
> —ROMANS 8:29

It's not heresy to want to be conformed with the image and likeness of Jesus Christ; it's your destiny! Moving toward Zion is what conforms you to the image of Jesus. There are a lot of people who don't know how to get to Zion, the place of reigning in the Christian life, the place of spiritual maturity. How do you get to Zion? You find a person who's

125

been there and you get them to show you the way. That's how you learn everything in life. This is what the Bible calls *discipleship*.

> How blessed is the man whose strength is in Thee; in whose heart are the highways to Zion!
> —PSALM 84:5, NAS

How did the children of Israel get through the wilderness? By following and having a relationship with a man who had spent forty years in that wilderness. Moses didn't know it, but when he escaped Pharoah's judgment by running to the wilderness, the forty years he spent there leading sheep were preparing him to lead a nation through the wilderness later.

Whatever is going on in your life right now God will use to prepare you for where you are going. So you better learn it well! God's way to train you for reigning is to discipline you under others. There is no such thing as a self-made man. God's way is to teach you by example, wisdom, and encouragement of other believers.

If I want to learn how to make money, I'm going to hang around somebody who makes a lot of money. I'm not going to hang around somebody who's broke! How about you? If I'm going to learn about healing, I'm going to go learn from somebody who does it well and is getting some good results. I'm going to learn about soul-winning from somebody who wins souls.

If you want to learn about having a good marriage, don't ask somebody who's in the middle of a divorce. Ask somebody with a good marriage what they've learned. To be a good parent, look around your church and observe which kids are well-behaved, on fire for God, and are laughing and enjoying life. Don't go seeking the advice of parents whose kids are hanging off the wall and running across the front, while they sit looking like they've been hit with a Flash Gordon ray gun or something!

> He that walketh with wise men shall be wise:
> but a companion of fools shall be destroyed.
> —PROVERBS 13:20

If I want to be a bricklayer I might read a book about it, but I won't become a bricklayer until I find a man who can teach me. I want to find a master bricklayer to apprentice under, someone who is excellent, faithful in natural things, meets the needs of others while he's in need, and is a covenant man. I will learn the skill of bricklaying by watching and doing it under a man who does it well.

Avoid friends who are not models of the truth. There are those who preach the doctrine of authority and submission, but they walk in rebellion. Some teach the Bible principles of prosperity and are always begging for money. Others talk success and exhibit nothing but failure.

We impart what we are, not what we say. You are not going to learn to be a good Christian from somebody who is not a good Christian. Why would you make somebody who walks in rebellion your best friend? That's nonsense! If my best friend suddenly goes bad, I'm going to do everything I can to restore him; but if he stays bad and tries to get me and my family to walk in rebellion with him, then

I'm going to have to break fellowship with him.

> Now I beseech you, brethren, mark them which cause divisions and offences contrary to the doctrine which ye have learned; and avoid them. For they that are such serve not our Lord Jesus Christ, but their own belly; and by good words and fair speeches deceive the hearts of the simple.
>
> —ROMANS 16:17–18

Do you know what *avoid* means? It means "a void" between you and someone else! Don't hang around people in rebellion or those who are practicing evil. Confront your brother or sister and provoke them to love and good works, but don't trust them or spend a lot of time with them until you see some good fruit begin to grow again.

You don't have to treat them as an enemy, because your separation from them is a loving, brotherly chastisement to bring them to repentance. Unfortunately most believers don't confront. They just shove things under the rug. They think they are covering their brother with love, but they are destroying him because of their ignorance.

They say, "Well, I know you've had five affairs in the church; you're down on everybody and disobedient to the Word; but we'll just go out and play a little racquetball together. We'll just pretend everything's fine." Real love says, "Sorry, we aren't playing anything together until you repent and get back in fellowship with the Lord and in covenant with the church."

In the Old Testament God rebuked Jehoshaphat

for helping Ahab. He said, "He's the worst guy I've ever had as king, so why are you allying yourself with him in a war? You almost got killed!" (See 2 Chronicles 18 and 19:2.)

You stay alive, and you get to Zion by learning from those who are totally sold-out to God, not by hanging around with fools who think they know better than God.

THE CITY OF GOD

> Great is the LORD, and greatly to be praised in the city of our God, in the mountain of his holiness. Beautiful for situation, the joy of the whole earth, is mount Zion, on the sides of the north, the city of the great King.
>
> —PSALM 48:1–2

Once Jerusalem was occupied by David and his mighty men it became the high place in Israel. The Bible says in many places that they went *up* to Jerusalem, whereas they went *down* to Jericho. From every place in Israel you had to go up to Jerusalem; you never went down.

Jerusalem became the seat of God's government in Israel. That's where the throne was, where the temple was, and where the rulership of God's king, David, was. It was the place of government and authority, and it was beautiful. Many Scriptures talk about Jerusalem as a place of beauty, and I believe the day is coming when God's kingdom, which means God's authority, will be beautiful.

You see, right now *authority* is a dirty word.

Government is a dirty word. If we spent as much effort and time beautifying our own governments as we do putting them down, we'd be in the Millennium by now! But we do nothing but criticize them and have not honored them.

The average Christian does not regard the government of his church as something beautiful either. Generally he looks down on it. So government is so busy defending itself that it has no time to lead. Its purpose and meaning has been lost.

However, just as the government of God was brought to the city of Jerusalem by David and his mighty men, Jesus is going to build His church as we bring our lives under the government of God. Then He will bring us to Zion, to the place of glory, victory, and reigning!

The Book of Hebrews depicts David's occupation of Zion as a picture of the church. The enemy had stolen the glory of God from the church and had driven us down off Zion. But now we're hearing the battle cry; we're hearing the Holy Spirit speak. As God restored natural Israel, He is going to restore spiritual Israel.

> But ye are come unto mount Sion, and unto the city of the living God, the heavenly Jerusalem, and to an innumerable company of angels.
> —HEBREWS 12:22

Legally, coming to Zion is a finished fact. Jesus has already done it. In Christ we have already come to the place of ruling and reigning. Nevertheless, we haven't come there *experientially*. We have to possess it! Unfortunately most of us live in spiritual suburbia, out on the plains where it's comfortable, and running into town—the city of God—when we need something or some evil befalls us.

Very few spend their lives moving closer and closer to Zion with the focus of their lives on ruling and reigning, which is spiritual maturity. Few understand and then make the choice to discipline themselves to live according to the Spirit, not satisfying the lusts of the flesh.

Most believers live in the flatlands, and when the floods come and their beautiful homes, built on sand, start to shake they suddenly feel the leading of the Lord to move up higher toward Zion. Why? Is it because they're so spiritual? No. It's because the devil just ripped the shirt off their back! Most of us get nudged up to Zion by agitation, pain, distress, circumstances, and trouble.

Whether you believe God sends trouble or not, trouble comes! And when it comes you have the choice to move closer to Zion or stay camped in the lowlands. Ultimately you will get kicked in the teeth enough to realize that the only safe place for you is to keep moving toward Zion, growing up to rule and reign.

According to Hebrews 12:22, the first thing you see when you come to Mount Zion is the city of the living God. This is not talking about heaven, streets of gold, pearly gates, and mansions. This is the church. *You are the city of God.*

> And I John saw the holy city, new Jerusalem, coming down from God out of heaven, prepared as a bride adorned for her husband.
> —REVELATION 21:2

That's not a town like New York City; that's the church, the bride of Christ!

When you come into the city of God, what do you find? An innumerable company of angels—not demons. The angels are there to protect you. When we come into the family of God, into the city of God, we come under divine protection. Protection is going to be one of the important things in this last day. If you stay in God's will you'll be under His protection.

> The angel of the LORD encampeth round about them that fear them, and delivereth them.
> —PSALM 34:7

Returning to the passage in Hebrews, chapter 12, we learn more about what we have come to when we come to Mount Zion.

> To the general assembly and church of the firstborn, which are written in heaven, and to God the Judge of all, and to the spirits of just men made perfect.
> —HEBREWS 12:23

Notice this verse says that just men are made perfect. God comes to live in our spirits, then begins the process of perfecting us or maturing us from the inside out. We come to Zion at the new birth in our spirits, but the full manifestation of living in Zion, ruling and reigning with Jesus Christ in our natural lives, comes as we are conformed to His image.

And to Jesus the mediator of the new covenant,

and to the blood of sprinkling, that speaketh
better things than that of Abel.

—HEBREWS 12:24

When we are born again, we come to Jesus and
enter into a New-Covenant relationship. They will
know us by how we love one another! We have a
superior covenant, which says better things to the
world around us.

We are conformed to the image of Jesus by
being faithful in natural things as unto the Lord
(Bethlehem), serving others as unto the Lord when
we ourselves are in desperate need (Adullam), and
committing ourselves to the integrity and compassion of walking in covenant with our brothers and
sisters in Christ (Hebron).

We pass through Bethlehem, Adullam, and then
Hebron in the structure and framework of discipleship. We begin by imitating and learning from those
who have been to Zion, and then we continue to be
conformed to His image by discipling others ourselves.

As every believer reproduces themselves many
times over, nothing can stand against us as we cor-
porately come to Zion. We are bringing the kingdom
and government of God into our hearts and minds,
into our homes, into our churches, and into the
entire body of Christ.

We are not trying to build the church, but if we
bring the kingdom into our lives the church will
come. The nearer we come to the throne, to the
place of ruling and reigning in Christ, the more we
are going to comprehend what the church is, and
the more we will see and comprehend how Jesus is
building His church.

The church is the city of God, and Jesus said He would build it. Our part is to make disciples. It seems that we're worrying about Jesus' business instead of our business! One day we're going to see the church, but it is not built yet. Jesus said, "I will build My church"—future tense—it is under construction.

When God gave Adam a wife in Genesis 2:22, the Hebrew says He "built" Eve, and she is a type of the church, the bride of Christ. I don't know if it took God twenty minutes or twenty years, but it was a process when He built Eve. In the same way Jesus is building the church today. It isn't finished yet. We don't see it in its full manifestation now, but one day we will. What we've done is make the church now and the kingdom later, when the church is still being built, but the kingdom has already come.

This is the concept of kingdom now. Hold on! I know some of you just felt your blood pressure go through the roof because I've brought up a controversial subject called "kingdom now." Therefore I want to be very clear about what I say here.

First, *kingdom* means "rule or authority." It's very simple. Second, if you are in the kingdom of God, you are subject to the rule, government, and authority of God. For example, the kingdom of Saudi Arabia means that when I get off the plane in Saudi Arabia I come under that government, authority, and rule.

Our purpose is to make disciples, and we cannot make disciples if we haven't first put our own lives in subjection to the government of God. You cannot show anyone else how to get to Zion if you haven't been there yourself.

The kingdom of God is in our hearts right now,

and His government is ruling in our spirits. This is why we are so compelled to get the sin out of our lives and carnality out of our relationships, get out of debt, build a foundation, and become a people of integrity. The Bible says judgment begins first with the house of God, and that's you and me.

> For the time is come that judgment must begin at the house of God: and if it first begin at us, what shall the end be of them that obey not the gospel of God?
>
> —1 PETER 4:17

God is not judging the world now; He's judging us. He's cleaning us up and purging us of anything that will not be subject to His kingdom. He's purifying the hearts of His people. He's manifesting what's in our hearts—pride, wrong motives, rebellion, selfish ambition—and calling us to repentance.

God wants all of us to come under His authority, under His government, which means being perfected and purged and cleansed and conformed to the image of Jesus. He wants to see "Christ in you the hope of glory."

There are two aspects to growing up in Christ that seem to be opposed to one another at first, but the more you grow up, the more you realize they are working together toward the same end. First, God wants us to be totally and unequivocally dependent upon Him. Our identity, worth, and purpose are to be found only in Him.

> I am crucified with Christ: nevertheless I live; yet not I, but Christ liveth in me: and the life

135

which I now live in the flesh I live by the faith
of the Son of God, who loved me, and gave
himself for me.

—GALATIANS 2:20

On the other hand, God didn't make us robots
either. He gave us a will, a mind to reason and
think with, and a heart filled with passion. He wants
our companionship and friendship. But an adult
and a baby cannot have an equal relationship. A
baby has to reach some level of maturity before it
can really converse and do things with an adult. So
too, God wants us to grow up.

We see the same principle in the natural. What if
my children never learned to brush their teeth, tie
their shoes, make their beds, or eat with a knife and
fork? We don't mind helping them while we're
teaching them, but it would be abnormal if our children never grew up and learned to do anything for
themselves.

The same is true in the church. If a new babe in
Christ saw a demon manifest and panicked, that
would be normal. However, if they have been
saved for several years, they should be at a place
where they know they have authority over the thing
and can command it to go in Jesus' name.

Still, you can't understand what it is to reign and
act and think like Jesus without being totally
immersed in Him. This is where these two principles come together to get you to grow up. First you
get rid of pride and realize you can't do all things,
except through Jesus Christ. Then you trust Him to
lead you, guide you, and empower you to rule and
reign.

You're dependent upon God, but you're mature in the knowledge of Jesus Christ. As a result you are thinking, speaking, and acting like Jesus. You are being conformed to His image.

Learning to reign is a process, not a quick fix. You have to grow up. If you're a baby Christian and you have just been saved, take your time. But for the rest of us that have been saved for a long time, how long are we going to stay children?

There are some things God won't do for us. We have to get up and do them for ourselves. For example, when the angel awakened Peter to let him out of jail the angel didn't tie Peter's sandals. Peter had to do that himself. The angel opened the door, but Peter had to walk out and go tell those who were praying that their prayers had been answered.

God isn't going to do everything for you either. He will open the door, and when you are obedient to walk through it He will anoint you, but you are still going to have to walk through that door yourself and go tell others about the new truth and freedom you are experiencing!

We'll *go up* when the time comes, but right now we need to spend all of our time and effort trying to *grow up*. We must become good fathers, good mothers, good husbands, good wives, good sons and daughters, good employees, and good friends.

Then, as we are faithful in both the natural things and the spiritual things, God will not withhold anything from us. We will have been trained and be ready to reign!